# The Best of AMISH COOKING

# The Best of
# AMISH
# COOKING

*Traditional and Contemporary
Recipes Adapted from the Kitchens
and Pantries of Old Order Amish Cooks*

## Phyllis Pellman Good

Intercourse, Pennsylvania 17534

## Acknowledgements and Credits

Many Old Order Amish friends and acquaintances delved into their memories and recipe boxes to answer hours of my questions. There is always work to be done, yet these folks sat patiently at their kitchen tables or on nearby sofas while I gathered facts, impressions and recipes. I am deeply grateful.

Still other friends provided the settings for photography in their kitchens and basements. The Hans Herr House, the oldest remaining home in Lancaster County, built in 1719 by a Mennonite leader, graciously allowed us to photograph the cover and several other shots on that property. Thank you all.

Design by Craig Heisey
Photography design by Kenneth Pellman
Photography by Jonathan Charles

THE BEST OF AMISH COOKING
Copyright © 1988 by Good Books, Intercourse, Pennsylvania 17534
International Standard Book Number: 0-934672-70-9
Library of Congress Catalog Card Number: 88-82138

### Library of Congress Cataloging-in-Publication Data

Good, Phyllis Pellman, 1948–
  The best of Amish cooking.

  Bibliography: p.
  Includes index.
  1. Cookery, Amish.   2. Cookery—Pennsylvania.
  I. Title.
  TX715.G647   1988        641.5′088287        88-82138
  ISBN 0-934672-70-9

# Table of Contents

# An Introduction to the Amish and Their Food

The Amish have captured the interest of the modern world because of their quaint clothing, homes and buggies, their striking quilts, their lusty food. These people prefer to be regarded as a community of faith who deliberately seek to live in a way that honors God and the creation. They purposely refuse many conveniences to better foster their life together; they choose to live close to the land in an effort to care for their families and the earth.

## Who Are These People?

The Amish are a Christian group who trace their beginnings to the time of the Protestant Reformation in 16th century Europe.

In 1525 a group of believers parted company with the established state church for a variety of reasons. Among them was the conviction that one must voluntarily become a follower of Christ, and that that deliberate decision will be reflected in all of one's life. Therefore, baptism must symbolize that choice. The movement was nicknamed "Anabaptism," meaning re-baptism, since the believers wanted to be baptized again as adults.

Eventually the group were called Mennonites after Menno Simons, one of their leaders who had formerly been a Roman Catholic priest. Over the years these people grew into a strong faith community, concerned with the nurture and discipline of each other.

Basic to their beliefs was a conviction that if one was a faithful follower of Christ's, one's behavior would clearly distinguish one from the larger world. These people saw themselves as separated unto God because of their values of love, forgiveness and peace. Because they were misunderstood and because they appeared to be a threat to the established church and government, the people were often persecuted and many became refugees.

In 1693, a magnetic young Mennonite leader believed that the church was losing some of its purity and that it was beginning to compromise with the world. And so he and a group who agreed with him left the Mennonites and formed a separate fellowship. They were called Amish, after their leader, Jacob Amman. Today the Amish identify themselves as the most conservative group of Mennonites.

The movement which Amman began reached into Switzerland, Alsace and the Palatinate area of Germany. As early as 1727 Amish families began to resettle in North America where they found farmland, space to live as neighbors to each other, and a climate that nurtured their growth as a church family with a distinctive lifestyle.

The tiny communities struggled to survive in the early years. As was true for other pioneers, the Amish invested most of their time and energy in clearing the land, establishing their homesteads and getting along with the native Americans. Most of those who arrived from the 1720s through the mid-1760s settled in eastern Pennsylvania, yet they did not live in sequestered communities. Frequently they had neighbors who were not Amish. With that came the opportunity for interchange with folks from the larger world. Nor was the Amish church as defined in terms of distinctive practices nor as organized under recognized leaders as it became following the American Revolution. That event crystallized many of the convictions these people held and united them in their refusal to join the War, since they were (and remain today) conscientious objectors.

The Amish intend to give their primary attention and energy to being faithful disciples of the teachings of Jesus Christ. They believe they can do that best as members of a community who together share that desire. Consequently they have tried to withstand acculturation into the "worldly" society surrounding them. They have remained close to the land, preferring to farm if at all possible. They believe hard work is honorable, that church and family provide one's primary identity. Their ideal in life is not to pursue careers that lead to prosperity and prestige, but to become responsible and contributing members to their faith community.

The Amish have changed throughout their nearly 300 years of history. Their intent, however, is to be deliberate about change, to manage it carefully so that it does not erode their convictions.

The Amish continue to grow. Today they live in 20 states and one Canadian province, totaling about 100,000 adults and children. There are twice as many Amish persons today as there were only 20 years ago. They are a living and dynamic people.

# What is Their Food Tradition in the New World?

Because they are highly disciplined, the Amish are often perceived as being grim, austere folks who live as ascetics. They do live ordered lives and, in general, are restrained in their outward expression. But in two particular areas they have exercised color — in their quilts and in their food! In both areas they distinguished themselves only after becoming established in North America. By the mid-1850s and during the next several decades a food tradition evolved that included an amalgam of dishes from a variety of sources: they brought their own cultural taste preferences from Switzerland and Germany; that affected what they copied and adapted from the diets of their English and native American neighbors; the geography and climate in the area of the New World where they made their homes also shaped their eating. In those ways, however, they were little different from the other German folk who settled in William Penn's colony.

How, then, did the Amish develop and retain a food tradition that is identifiable? With their sustained rural base, the Amish have continued a productive relationship with their gardens and fields. With their large extended families they have not only been able to convey the love of certain dishes to their children, but they have also been able to show their daughters how to make those specialties, many of which are learned best by "feel" than by reading a cookbook. In addition, their active community life supports the continuation of a food tradition — at gathered times, favorite dishes appear, undergirding the event, whether it be a school picnic, a funeral, or sisters' day.

Several principles prevail among these people with as much strength now as they did when the first Amish built their homestead in Pennsylvania: to waste is to destroy God's gift. To be slack, work-wise, is to be disrespectful of time and resources. To go hungry is to ignore the bounty of the earth (furthermore, there is no reason that eating shouldn't be a pleasure!).

Many myths exist about these people and their food. Separated as the Amish are from the larger world in their dress and transportation choices, they are not immune to the many food options in the grocery stores of their communities. They shop, and so they pick up packaged cereal, boxes of fruit-flavored gelatin and cans of concentrated soup. Although tuna noodle casserole and chili con carne turn up on the tables of Amish homes, and chocolate chip cookies and lunch meat are packed into the lunch boxes of Amish school children, cornmeal mush and chicken pot pie are still favorites. Because the Amish are a living group, despite their regard for tradition, their menus continue to change. Their foods are influenced by their neighbors and the recipes they find on boxes containing packaged foods or in the pages of farm magazines and local newspapers.

The Amish are hard workers whose efforts on the land have been rewarded with fruitful fields and gardens. And so they have eaten well. In fact, their land has been so productive that Amish cooks have undertaken massive "pickling" operations, preserving the excess from their gardens in sweet and sour syrups. Likely one amazed guest, who sat at the table of an Amish cook or who witnessed her well-stocked canning shelves, began the tale of "seven sweets and seven sours." That exaggeration of what is typically served has a bit of truth at its core — hard work has its payoff and all food is made to be enjoyed.

Desserts are eaten daily in most Amish homes. But multiple desserts at one meal are generally eaten only when there is company. Thus the story of manifold pastries available at every meal has only a shade of truth in it.

## What Does this Cookbook Contain?

This cookbook is a collection of those dishes that go back as far as 80-year-old members of the Amish church can recall or discover in hand-written "cookbooks" which belonged to their mothers, and that are still prepared today, either in the old-fashioned way or by an adapted method. These foods are ones that were — and still are — eaten (perhaps now in a modified form), in eastern Pennsylvania, most often in the Lancaster area. It was in that general community that the first Amish settlements took root and grew. Although Lancaster gave birth to many daughter colonies, it is today the second largest Amish community (Holmes County, Ohio, is the largest).

Typically those hand-written and food-spattered cookbooks included only ingredients without any, or only minimal, reference to procedures. Furthermore, the measurements were far from precise! Most Amish folks recall that their mothers seldom consulted a cookbook anyway. Experience kept their skills polished. In keeping with the Amish tradition of living as extended families, an elderly mother or aunt was usually nearby to offer help.

*The Best of Amish Cooking* contains old recipes, but they are written to be understood and used by those without the benefit of these people's history or the presence of an experienced cook. Recipe sizes have also been adapted, in most cases to yield six to ten servings.

Throughout the book, pronoun references to the cook in Amish homes are consistently of the feminine gender. That was done deliberately, since in Amish society, roles are clearly defined. Women are solely responsible for food preparation, apart from butchering and related processes such as drying and smoking, certain gardening chores, and making apple or pear butter. A man who carries primary responsibilities in the kitchen is a rare exception.

Here, then, is the possibility of making good food — not fancy, but substantial; more hearty than delicate; in tune with the seasons.

# Mainstays and One-Pot Dishes

History and convenience have worked hand in hand in the creation of many mainstays in the typical Amish diet. Both pleasure and tradition have established these dishes as favorites over the years, in one form or another.

Many one-pot meals trace their beginnings to open-hearth cooking when the primary food for a meal went into a kettle suspended over the fire. When ranges replaced fireplaces in the mid-1800s, certain dishes survived that modernization of kitchen equipment. In many cases the combination of flavors in a dish was particularly pleasing — chicken pot pie, for example; in others, the ingredients happened to be available during the same season of the year — such as pork and sauerkraut. There were still other dishes which fit the family farm schedule and so became mainstays — cornmeal mush, for instance.

Cornmeal mush is a cousin to the hasty pudding of the 19th century. Its roots may be traced still further back to the European porridge, originally eaten as a bread substitute. That staple, blended with the American Indian corn tradition, was taken one step further in its development by the German folk who made their home in eastern Pennsylvania. These settlers distinguished their mush from the cornmeal dishes made elsewhere in the country by roasting the yellow field corn in a bakeoven (and later in a range) before it was shelled and ground at the mill. The roasting process gave a nutty rich flavor to the cornmeal.[1] Mush persists today in the diet of the Old Order Amish.

Pot pies, which typically use wheat flour in their noodles, also have their origins in the one-pot stews of open-hearth cooking. Meat, vegetables, broth and a tasty extender could simmer, with little attention from the cook.

Large families and unannounced company tutored many Amish cooks in making meals go far. Noodles (or their cousins, dumplings and rivvels) could be tossed into bubbling broth and stretch the stew. Wheat flourished in eastern Pennsylvania, so wheat flour was available for cooking and baking. Many farms had a flock of chickens, so eggs were easily at hand. Noodles came to be a favorite and frequently made side dish or main ingredient.

These traditional dishes, in contrast to many more modern casseroles, begin with sturdy ingredients that generally improve with long slow cooking. Ham with green beans, and pork and sauerkraut have long histories with Amish cooks. Other combinations have been retained but adapted—for example, baked stuffed pig stomachs brown appetizingly in the oven.

Still other favorite mainstays have developed as quickie parallels to the satisfaction provided by those meals that brewed for hours. Stewed crackers with eggs are routinely eaten for breakfast in Amish homes. On the other hand, stewed crackers with oysters or pink salmon became a traditional company dish. One Amish historian remembers that stewed chicken and gravy over homemade crackers was the main dish served at their weddings during the Depression years.

Fried crackers are remembered fondly by the older people as a welcome side dish for the main meal. Eliminate saltines or oyster crackers from the grocery store and the Amish will have lost a basic ingredient for many nearly instant yet basic dishes.

The following recipes, which grew out of strenuous times, still fit well in a household where the cook juggles extensive homemaking duties, child-rearing, gardening, and often, barn or field work.

# Chicken Pie

"My grandmother at Christmas time would make chicken pie and oyster pie. And my mother holds to that too. That's still the main meal for the family at Christmas."

*Filling*

1 fat hen, cooked until tender
3 Tbsp. butter
3 Tbsp. flour
5 cups chicken broth
1 cup milk
2 – 3 cups cooked potatoes, peas and carrots, mixed together

Remove chicken from bones. Cut meat into bite-sized pieces. Set aside. Melt butter; stir in flour. Blend in chicken broth and milk, and cook until smooth and slightly thickened. Add chicken to gravy.

Spread vegetables on bottom of greased baking pan. Pour chicken gravy over top.

*Crust*

2 cups flour
2 tsp. baking powder
1 tsp. salt
2 Tbsp. chicken fat or shortening
1 cup milk
1 egg

Mix dry ingredients together. Cut in shortening until mixture resembles peas. Stir in milk and mix well. Add egg and blend. Roll out dough, then spread over chicken. Cut slits in dough to permit steam to escape. Bake at 425° for 20 – 30 minutes or until crust is brown.

# Chicken Pot Pie

Chicken Pot Pie is a stew cooked on top of the stove. It usually includes cut-up potatoes and is seasoned with chopped onions. Pot pie noodles "are cut thicker and used right away," in contrast to noodles that are eaten as a side dish (which must dry before being cooked). "Pot pie has more body. They aren't just slippery noodles," explains one Amish man.

An Amish grandmother remembers, "Mom liked to make chicken pot pie whenever we had men for silo filling or haymaking. We always had chickens, so she'd kill a few in the morning and we'd have them for lunch. Whenever we had unexpected company we could go kill a chicken!

"Chicken pot pie is a meat-saving dish. Now it's not a quick thing. Mom always had onions and potatoes to put in. And she'd make the pot pie noodles right then. She didn't keep a supply of them on hand. When I make pot pie I put in some carrots, too, for flavor and color. It's a good meal to make when our children come to visit."

Personal touches are a part of all these dishes. "I put a few threads of saffron in my pot pie," explained another Amish grandmother. "It adds a little color and flavor."

> 1 3½-4 lb. chicken
> 4 medium-sized potatoes, peeled and cut into chunks
> 1 onion, diced
> salt and pepper to taste
> pot pie squares

Cook the chicken in two quarts water until it is partly tender. Then add the onion and potatoes and cook until they and the chicken are completely tender. Remove meat from bones and set aside.

Bring broth to a boil. Drop pot pie squares into boiling broth and cook 20 minutes or until tender. Return chicken to the broth and serve steaming hot.

> *Pot Pie Dough*
>
> 2 eggs
> 2 cups flour

2 – 3 Tbsp. milk or cream

Break the eggs into the flour. Work together, adding the milk or cream to make a soft dough. Roll out the dough as thin as possible and cut into 1″ × 2″ rectangles with a knife or pastry wheel. Drop into boiling broth.

# Chicken Roast

Roast is a crowd pleaser. Today it is the main dish served at Old Order Amish weddings in Lancaster County. It has been so for many years.

Some families make roast for Christmas dinner. Others traditionally prepared it for threshers.

Roast has the qualifications for being a favorite in the Amish community for cook and feasters alike. Its ingredients are readily available; the combination of flavors is basic and full-bodied; it can be prepared with turkey or duck if the supply — or taste preferences of those eating — so demand.

> 1½ loaves homemade bread
> 1 lb. butter or margarine
> 1½ tsp. salt
> ½ tsp. pepper
> 1 tsp. celery seed
> ¾ cup celery, chopped (optional)
> meat from a whole chicken, stewed and removed from bones

Crumble the bread by hand into a large mixing bowl. Melt the butter; then pour it over the bread crumbs. Add the seasonings and chopped celery. Then mix with the deboned chicken chunks.

Turn into a large roast pan and bake covered at 350° for a half hour to an hour, until heated through. Dampen with water around the edge if it begins to dry out. Stir often to prevent sticking.

*Note:* You may make a rich gravy to serve over the roast by thickening the chicken broth with flour.

# Pork and Sauerkraut

Fresh pork became available after fall butchering. In the days preceding freezers, fresh meat was eaten promptly or canned for later use.

Sauerkraut was also an autumn dish. Late harvested cabbage was shredded and stomped into sauerkraut, then served as a vegetable through the cold months when the garden was not productive.

Today, although canning and freezing make pork and sauerkraut a possible meal at any time of the year, it is still thought of as a dish most appropriately eaten when there is a chill in the air. Served usually with mashed potatoes, pork and sauerkraut is a combination of balanced tastes — the sharp, acidic quality offsetting the rich pork.

**4 – 6 lb. fresh pork roast or 3 – 4 lbs. spare ribs**
**salt and pepper to taste**
**1 quart sauerkraut**

Season meat. Place in roaster, add ½ cup water and cover with lid. Bake at 350° for 2½ – 3 hours.

Add sauerkraut around roast or ribs. Cover with lid and return to oven. Continue baking at 350° for an additional hour.

# Ham and Green Beans

Smoked hams hung in the attic from one fall's butchering until the next. When the supply was strong, ham and green beans could be made with a smoked shoulder or picnic. As the number and size of the meat cuts dwindled, ham and green beans could still be made, although it was more likely prepared with a ham butt, primarily for flavoring.

Green beans were dried and in later years canned—for use throughout the winter months, and so this dish developed as a sort of tasty and logical combination. The unnamed, but expected ingredient in this meal was potatoes, often cut up in chunks rather than mashed.

A customary side dish was cole slaw (see page 80). Its vinegar dressing provided the "bite" to offset the heavier meat. Furthermore, cabbage kept well into the spring and so was handy for this wintry meal.

Although much time had already been spent in butchering and curing the ham, in picking and preserving the green beans and in digging the potatoes, the immediate preparation of this meal was relatively quick and easy for the cook.

> 2 – 3 lb. ham shoulder or picnic or 1 – 2 lb. ham hock
> 4 potatoes, peeled and cut in chunks
> 1 quart green beans

Place the ham in a roaster, add ½ cup water and cover. Bake at 350° for 1 – 1½ hours.

Add potatoes and green beans to roaster. Cover and return to oven for an additional hour of baking.

This can also be cooked on top of the stove. Place the ham in a heavy kettle. Add 2 inches of water and cook slowly, covered, for 1½ hours. Add potatoes and green beans and continue cooking slowly for another hour, or until the meat is tender and the potatoes are soft.

# Stuffed Pig Stomach

"We always expected a pig stomach at butchering time. That was special."

Stuffing a pig stomach with a sausage-potato-onion mix is a blend of the innovation and conviction against wastefulness that characterizes the Amish.

The texture of the browned, chewy skin against the moist richness of sausage and cubed potatoes has made this combination survive the demise of family butchering. Today, thanks to freezers, pig stomachs are available from retail pork butchers in the Lancaster area at almost any time of the year.

One gray-haired Amish man recalls that his mother "put oysters in pig stomach instead of sausage." A middle-aged woman remembers that at serving time, her mother "would take the stuffing out of the stomach, grind the skin, then lay that meat over the stuffing. She did that because the skin was not evenly browned and it was not of equal thickness. That way no one felt cheated for getting a thin spot and no one got stuck with a too chewy piece!"

> 1 large, well cleaned pig stomach
> 1½ lbs. bulk sausage meat
> 6 medium potatoes, peeled and diced
> 1 small onion, chopped

Cook potatoes and onion together until potatoes are tender. Separate sausage meat into small pieces and add to potato mixture. Stir and cook only until sausage loses its reddish color.

Drain off excess liquid. Stuff mixture loosely into stomach and close all openings with skewers laced with string. Place in roast pan with ½ cup water. Place remaining mixture that will not fit in stomach in a buttered casserole.

Cover roast pan containing the stomach and bake at 350° for 2–2½ hours. After first hour prick stomach with sharp fork. Place casserole of remaining mixture in oven, uncovered, and bake only for the last 40–45 minutes of baking time.

Overstuffing the stomach may cause it to burst while baking, because the stomach shrinks considerably.

*Makes 4 servings*

# Meat Pie

   2 – 3 cups cooked beef
   3 – 4 cups cooked vegetables (potatoes, peas, carrots,
      onions or other leftovers)
   2 – 3 cups gravy

Layer meat and vegetables into 3-quart baking dish or two
pastry-lined pie plates.

Pour gravy over mixture or prepare thickened broth by
melting 2 Tbsp. margarine. Stir in 2 Tbsp. flour, 1 tsp. salt and
⅛ tsp. pepper. When blended, gradually add 2 cups beef broth
and 1 cup milk. Bring to boil, stirring until thickened.

Cover baking dish or pie plates with pie crust. Cut slits in
crust to allow steam to escape.

Bake at 425° for 35 minutes. Turn off oven but let pie sit in it
for 10 – 15 minutes so that the flavors can blend.

   *Pie Crust (makes 4 crusts)*

   3 cups flour
   1 tsp. salt
   1¼ cups vegetable shortening
   1 egg, beaten
   ⅓ cup cold water
   1 Tbsp. vinegar

Mix flour and salt. Cut in shortening. Combine remaining
ingredients and stir into shortening mixture. Let stand a few
minutes.

Roll dough on floured board to desired thickness.

# Oyster Pie

"Oyster pie was always a treat, although we had it maybe once a month. An oyster man came around regularly and he'd give a lot more juice with the oysters than you get in the store!"

Only sixty miles from Philadelphia, the Lancaster area had easy access to the fish and oyster trade flowing through the seaport city. In fact, Lancaster farmers sold their wheat, which they raised primarily as a cash crop during the mid- to late 1800s, in Philadelphia. Or they took their potatoes to Reading where, by way of the canal system, they were sent on to Philadelphia. In addition to seafood, lemons, oranges and bananas found their way to Lancaster tables.

> 4 cups potatoes, cooked and cubed
> ¼ cup celery, chopped
> 1 pint oysters with liquor
> 2 eggs, hardboiled and cut up
> 1 tsp. salt
> ¼ tsp. pepper
> 2 Tbsp. butter
> 1½ cups milk

Alternate layers of potatoes, celery, oysters, eggs and seasonings in baking pan. Dot with butter. Pour milk and oyster liquor over.

*Crust*

> 1½ cups flour
> ½ tsp. salt
> ½ cup plus 2 Tbsp. shortening
> 1 egg, beaten
> 2 Tbsp. cold water
> 1½ tsp. vinegar

Mix flour and salt. Cut in shortening.
Combine egg, water and vinegar and stir into shortening mixture. Refrigerate for a few minutes.
Roll out dough on floured board. Place over oyster mixture.

Cut slits in dough to permit steam to escape. Bake at 375° for 45 minutes.

# Oysters with Bread Filling

This is a sturdy, yet special meal that is less laborious than the preparation of fried oysters. One does need forethought to get this dish fixed by mealtime, however.

Oysters with bread filling can be adapted to the size of the crowd at the table. This recipe, in the words of one who has made the dish frequently, allows the cook some latitude. But be warned by the wisdom of an experienced oysters-with-bread-filling baker, "Don't worry about having leftovers. Just be sure you make *enough!*"

> white or whole wheat bread, sliced
> butter or margarine
> oysters with liquor
> milk
> salt and pepper

The day before serving the filling, cut the bread up into ¾ inch cubes. Pile them in a dishpan, then cover it with a tea towel so the bread dries out a bit, but not too much.

The next day melt butter and margarine (use about 1 cup to a pound loaf of bread) in a larger pan. Remove half of it and set aside. Add bread cubes to the butter in the pan. Pour the reserved butter over the cubes and stir. Continue stirring the bread over heat until it browns but doesn't burn.

Take a long shallow pan and cover the bottom of it with one-half of the browned bread cubes. Follow that with a layer of 1 – 1½ dozen oysters (either whole or cut up), then the remaining bread cubes and another 1 – 1½ dozen oysters.

Pour the oyster liquid, mixed with ¼ – ½ cup milk, over the bread and oysters. The filling should be damp throughout, but not soggy or wet. (Add more milk if it seems too dry or more bread if it's gotten too wet.) Salt and pepper to taste.

Bake uncovered at 275° – 300° until the filling is heated through (stir it up to check) and slightly browned on top.

# Homemade Noodles

Noodles became a specialty of the German settlers in Pennsylvania. They brought with them a taste for the dish. It was in the rich farmland of the mid-Atlantic area of the New World, however, that wheat flourished as it hadn't in Europe. Here the people had access to wheat flour. Many farms also had their own flock of chickens and, thus, the eggs needed to make the rich dough.

One Amish woman in her early 40s explains, "Having your own eggs makes it easier to make your own noodles and pot pie. A lot of the older people want noodles at the main meal each day because they used to make them weekly." An older man agrees, "We always had homemade noodles. Some places today they don't have any chickens — they have big dairies instead — so they have to buy their noodles."

In some families, noodlemaking had a seasonal aspect. One woman, born in the 1920s, recalls, "If we had a lot of eggs, we'd make a lot of noodles. In the spring, when the chickens were older, the egg shells weren't as strong, so we'd have many 'cracks.' Then we'd mix up noodles, using the egg yolks. I would come home from school and see the noodles drying. I knew that somewhere there were egg whites, waiting to be made into chocolate angel food cake (see page 140)!"

Today's cooks need to weigh the matchless flavor of homemade noodles, yet the heavy time investment they require, against the inexpensive store-bought noodles that are so easily had. In most Amish homes, made-from-scratch noodles are a treat rather than a regularly served dish.

> 6 egg yolks
> 6 Tbsp. water
> 3 cups flour (approximately)
> ½ tsp. salt

Beat the egg yolks and water together thoroughly. Stir in the salt and flour to make a very stiff, yet workable dough.

Divide the dough into four balls. Roll each one out, making as thin a layer as possible. Lay each on a separate cloth to dry.

When they are dry enough not to stick together, stack them on top of each other and cut them lengthwise into thin strips.

Then cut across the width of the dough to form thin strips, about 1½ – 2 inches long.

Allow noodles to dry completely before storing them in an airtight container.

*Makes 1 pound*

*To Serve Homemade Noodles:*

Bring 3 quarts of water to a boil. Add 1½ Tbsp. salt and ½ lb. homemade noodles. Stir frequently. After water returns to boil, cook for 8 – 10 minutes. Drain and serve, covered with brown butter.

*Note:* Brown butter is a simple, yet pleasing topping for cooked noodles. It is a tradition practiced widely by Amish cooks, especially for use with noodles and steamed vegetables.

Melt desired amount of butter in saucepan. Allow it to brown (watch carefully so it doesn't burn). Pour over noodles in their serving dish.

# Wafers

Traditionally wafers were made to be served with creamed or stewed chicken. The combination was frequently the main dish served at wedding suppers.

**2 cups flour**
**¼ tsp. salt**
**1 tsp. sugar**
**½ tsp. baking powder**
**½ cup lard**
**1 egg**
**milk**

Mix dry ingredients together. Cut in lard until the mixture resembles small peas.

Stir in egg. Add milk, one tablespoon at a time, until the dough is damp and sticks together sufficiently to be rolled out as pie dough.

Roll thin. Place on cookie sheets and cut into 1″ squares or diamonds. Prick with fork. Bake at 350° just until brown.

Cool, then store in airtight container.

# Cornmeal Mush

Mush is one dish that has survived from the colonial days with little change or adaptation. Filling and satisfying, it is still eaten on winter mornings in many Amish households.

Although most mush is made now from store-bought, roasted cornmeal, traditionally the corn was roasted at home. In the fall, choice ears of field corn were picked and cleaned, then put into the bakeoven for roasting when the bread- and pie-baking was finished. In later years it was roasted in the cookstove, although that stove was much smaller than the bakeoven, casting some doubt on the efficiency of such an operation.

One Amish grandfather remembers, "We would dry the corn on the roof of one of the out-buildings, then bring it in to roast in the oven of the cookstove. We would shell it after it got to be a nice brown, either with a corn sheller or by hand as we sat around in the evening." The shelled kernels were taken to a mill to be ground into cornmeal flour.

Mush is eaten in two forms. The first is when it is pudding-like, immediately after it has boiled to the proper thickness. Family tradition and personal preference determine the time of day when it is eaten and what one mixes with it. Said one, "At home we ate mush for lunch – thick with sugar or molasses and milk. We used to dip our spoons into the molasses, then drain it off over the mush, trying to write words with the molasses!" Said another, "We always had mush in the evening, before it 'set up,' with milk and brown sugar."

After it cools for several hours, mush can be sliced and fried. Some families made a batch big enough to last for several days. "We'd eat the first mush on Mondays for supper. Then we would have it fried the rest of the week for breakfast."

Mush in this form is seldom eaten alone. "For breakfast we often had mush and puddin's (see page 49). And fried potatoes with an egg scrambled in the middle." But the cook in a non-dairy farm family explained, "I make mush and eggs in the evening because we don't milk cows here. So we aren't that hungry in the morning, and it feels better to eat that kind of thing in the evening. For us it's a winter meal, for a change, at suppertime."

Some old-time mush-eaters like horseradish with each bite of fried mush. Others prefer ketchup, while others choose molasses.

1 quart cold water
1 quart boiling water
2 cups roasted yellow cornmeal
1 tsp. salt

Put the cold water in a bowl. Combine the cornmeal and salt and stir into the cold water.

Bring the other quart of water to a boil. Slowly add the cornmeal and cold water mixture to it, stirring constantly to prevent lumps.

When smooth, cover and cook slowly for 1–3 hours, so the mush "glops" slowly. Stir frequently to keep from sticking to bottom of pan.

Serve.

Pour balance into loaf pans to mold. Let set until cool. Place in refrigerator for several hours until it is fully congealed.

Cut into ¼-inch thick slices and fry in margarine, butter or lard until brown. Turn and brown on the other side until crisp.

Serve.

# Steamed Crackers

Some Amish cooks make their own crackers, but those are used primarily as a base for stewed chicken and gravy. The crackers that turn up in those favorite Amish mainstays — Steamed (or Stewed) Crackers and Fried Crackers — are pre-packaged, boxed and bought at the store.

Hearty breakfasts and "snack meals" need variety. That fact, plus the cook's frequent obligation to produce a quick, yet stick-to-the-ribs meal are the likely backgrounds of these old favorites. Perhaps the Depression years also had a part in contributing these dishes to the Amish diet.

Sometimes steamed crackers are a full course; sometimes they are a side dish. Certain combinations have prevailed. "We had stewed crackers with eggs for breakfast." "We had stewed crackers with pink salmon for company as a side dish. I also remember stewed crackers with chicken. That was a main hot dish at weddings during the Depression."

¼–½ lb. (about 50–60) saltine crackers
2½ cups milk
2 Tbsp. butter or margarine
¾ cup milk

Butter the bottom and sides of a 1½ quart casserole. Lay dry crackers in the casserole. Heat the 2½ cups milk to scalding. Pour over crackers. Cover casserole and let stand at least 5 minutes, checking once to make sure the crackers are in the milk.

Just before serving, heat the butter until browned. Add ¾ cup milk and warm it. Then pour over the crackers.

*Makes 4–5 servings*

*Variations:*
1. Mix pieces of cooked pink salmon with the crackers as they are layered into the casserole. Proceed with recipe.
2. Mix small pieces of cooked chicken with the crackers as they are layered into the casserole. Proceed with recipe.
3. While crackers are standing, prepare 4 fried eggs in skillet. When crackers are finished serve into 4 dinner plates. Top each with a fried egg.

# Fried Crackers

An older Amish man, now widowed, explains another cracker specialty, "Sometimes when I make stewed crackers I use Trenton oyster crackers. You have to soak them for several hours until they expand. I make plenty, then fry whatever is left over in margarine!"

An Amish mother in her mid-thirties recalls her grandmother's procedure for the dish, "She used to buy very hard oyster crackers, soak them in boiling water to let them soften and expand, drain the water off, and fry them in butter on both sides. If she had company for supper she would often make them. And if she made them, she'd often make baked beans, too."

# Soups and Stews

Soups make a meal in the Amish world. Soups are not served as appetizers, nor are they prepared for the main meal of the day. They do, frequently, anchor the lunch or provide a snack, especially if there is fresh fruit in season.

Drawing upon their European soup tradition, which was especially strong in the Palatinate area of Germany, the early German settlers in Pennsylvania found soup a meal that translated well to the open-hearth cooking of the New World. The productive land and nurturing climate made meats, milk, butter and eggs more available than in Europe. Here, too, were an abundance of vegetables and fruits that offered seasonal varieties to the cook who prepared three full meals a day for a working family.

Although each cook concocts her own peculiar seasonings and special additions to the basic soups, certain qualities are common to those traditional stews prepared by Amish cooks. Most are thickened either by a roux or the addition of rivvels, crackers or bread. (Rivvels are made from flour and eggs—some cooks add salt and milk—which are rubbed together to form crumbs, then dropped into boiling broth. Rivvels are related to spaetzle, the German noodles which are native to the Swabian area of southwest Germany.)

Most soups are simple fare, made from whatever can be pulled most handily from the garden, canning shelves or root cellar. In that way they are an index to the food grown on an Amish homestead. From the bread and berries which go into Cold Soup to the stewing hen and corn which make up Chicken Corn Soup, the ingredients are nearly all native to the homeplace. The cook's schedule most likely determines whether she feeds her family Bean Soup or Vegetable Beef Stew.

Chicken Pot Pie (page 16)

Apple Dumplings (page 168)

# Potato Soup

Potato Soup still tops the list as the most frequently eaten soup in Amish homes. Some eat it with rivvels; others flavor it with chopped celery and onions. And although what accompanies the soup varies, the basic ingredients are the same.

"We grew our own potatoes, so we ate potato soup more than once a week. With it we would often have scrambled eggs, usually in sandwiches, because we grew our own chickens. It's a combination we still eat," said one mother in her early 40s.

"When we were first married we'd often have for Saturday dinner, potato soup — and schnitz pie in the left hand. A bite of one and then a bite of the other!" smiled an older man. That, too, is a widespread tradition. A woman in her mid-fifties remembered, "We used to say you couldn't have your piece of schnitz pie until you were on your second bowl of potato soup. My husband doesn't agree with that! He says you eat your pie right away!"

  3–4 potatoes, peeled and diced
  ¼ cup celery, chopped
  1½ cups water
  2 Tbsp. butter or margarine
  1 quart milk
  1 Tbsp. parsley
  salt and pepper to taste
  2 hardboiled eggs, diced

Cook the potatoes and celery in the water and butter until tender. Then add the milk, seasonings and eggs and heat thoroughly.

*Makes 6 servings*

# Creamy Potato Soup

3 Tbsp. butter
1 onion, diced
4 large potatoes, cubed
3 Tbsp. parsley, chopped
3 stalks celery and leaves, chopped
2 large carrots, chopped or grated
2 tsp. salt
¼ tsp. paprika
1½ cups boiling water
white sauce

Saute onion in butter until tender. Add remaining ingredients except white sauce and cook until vegetables are tender.
Add white sauce and stir until blended.

*Makes 6 Servings*

*White Sauce*

4 Tbsp. butter or margarine
2 Tbsp. flour
1 tsp. salt
¼ tsp. pepper
4 cups milk

Melt butter or margarine. Stir in flour and seasonings. When smooth, add milk and stir constantly until thickened.

# Potato Soup with Rivvels

¼ cup butter or margarine
10 – 12 potatoes, peeled and diced
salt and pepper
rivvels (see page 35)

Melt butter. Add potatoes, salt and pepper. Cover with water. Bring to a boil and cook potatoes until nearly soft.
Crumble in rivvels and continue cooking, stirring occasionally

so that rivvels separate.

When potatoes are tender, serve.

*Makes 6 – 8 servings*

# Rivvel Soup

Either rivvels, noodles, crackers or a white sauce have usually been mixed into the soups served at the kitchen tables of Amish households. There is a strong preference for starch in the food tradition of these people.

Rivvels are used in different ways. In one home the custom was this: "My mother made them in broth or water, then fished them out when they were cooked through and we'd put them into whatever soup we were eating, to make it go further."

In another home, "We usually made just Rivvel Soup — rivvels in milk with melted butter — rather than putting rivvels in other things."

> **2 Tbsp. butter or margarine**
> **2 quarts milk or meat stock**
> **rivvels**

Brown butter or margarine in a 3-quart soup pan. Add milk and bring to the boiling point. Crumble rivvels in slowly, stirring constantly until soup returns to a boil.

*Makes 4 servings*

> *Rivvels*
>
> **¾ cup flour**
> **1 egg**

Put flour in bowl. Break in egg and mix with a fork until dry and crumbly.

# Bean Soup

"We ate lots of bean soup; we grew our own 'Lazy Wife Beans.' They would be planted at the edge of the cornfield so they'd grow up the stalks and get plenty of sun. That way you didn't have to cut your own poles! But now you can't do that because they spray the corn.

"Bean soup was often our Saturday noon meal—with schnitz pie! It was an easy meal. The beans could cook while you cleaned. The pie, of course, had been made the day before."

> 1 cup navy beans, cooked
> ¼ cup water
> salt and pepper
> 3 quarts milk
> about ½ loaf stale bread, torn into bite-sized pieces
> 2–3 Tbsp. butter or margarine, browned

Bring cooked beans and water to boil in soup pan. Add seasonings to taste. Pour in milk and bring to boiling point. Stir in bread. Pour browned butter over.

*Makes 6–8 servings*

*To cook dried navy beans:*

Soak for 8 hours overnight in water (4 cups water to 1 cup dried beans).

Bring beans to boil in soaking water. Cover. Simmer for approximately 3 hours or longer if needed.

# Tomato Soup
## with celery, peppers and carrots

Some Amish cooks can a pulpy tomato juice, so laden with vegetables that their tomato soup requires no additional thickening.

>    1 pint tomato juice cocktail
>    scant ¼ cup water
>       ("Just enough to rinse out the jar!")
>    ⅛ tsp. baking soda
>    ¼ cup milk

Heat juice and water to the boiling point. Stir soda in carefully, watching that the mixture doesn't boil over.
Add milk and heat, but don't boil.

*Makes 3 servings*

*Tomato Juice Cocktail*

>    ½ bushel tomatoes
>    3 stalks celery (leaves and all)
>    3 large onions
>    6 medium carrots
>    3 green peppers
>    a little water
>    1 cup sugar
>    2 Tbsp. salt

Cut raw vegetables into 1-inch pieces. Put all together into large stockpot. Add water to a depth of 1 inch. Cook slowly until soft, then put through food press.

To pureed mixture add sugar and salt. Bring to a boil. Pour into jars and seal.

# Tomato Soup

Cooks who use a thin tomato juice for their soup generally use flour to give more body to the old favorite.

1 Tbsp. onion, minced
2 Tbsp. butter or margarine
3 Tbsp. flour
2 tsp. sugar
1 tsp. salt
dash of pepper
1 quart tomato juice
2 cups milk

Cook onion in butter until tender. Stir in flour and seasonings.
Blend in 2 cups tomato juice over heat. When smooth blend in remainder of juice. Bring to a boil, stirring constantly.
Meanwhile, heat milk to scalding. Then slowly add milk to tomato mixture and heat thoroughly, stirring frequently to blend and prevent sticking.

*Makes 4 – 6 servings*

# Hamburger Vegetable Soup

2 Tbsp. butter or margarine
1 onion, chopped
1 lb. hamburger
1½ tsp. salt
1 cup carrots, diced
½ cup celery, chopped
1 cup potatoes, diced
2 cups tomato juice
2 cups milk
¼ cup flour

Brown meat and onion in butter. Add remaining ingredients except milk and flour and cook until vegetables are tender.
Combine milk and flour and stir until smooth. Add to soup and cook until thickened.

*Makes 4 – 6 servings*

# Vegetable Beef Soup

"My mother cooked from the garden. Usually she put in our soup whatever she had a lot of, plus a beef bone to give it flavor. Now the women use a lot of hamburger."

The ingredients vary according to the day and season. Some Amish cooks can gallon jars of vegetable soup. It's a way to avoid wasting what can't be eaten as food grows in excess in bountiful gardens. It's also a deposit against drop-in company or a hectic day when housework interferes with food preparation.

The seasoning in soups, as well as most warm dishes eaten by the Amish, is usually limited to salt and pepper. If any ingredient is added to the vegetables, meats and milk, it is most often sugar. In general, people prefer mild food; one spicy exception is the wide use of horseradish, especially with meats.

    1 beef soup bone
    1½ tsp. salt
    2 quarts water
    2 cups potatoes, peeled and diced
    2 cups carrots, sliced
    1 cup celery, chopped
    1 cup cabbage, shredded
    2 cups peas
    2 cups green beans
    2 cups lima beans
    2 cups corn
    2 cups tomatoes or tomato juice
    ½ cup rice

Cook soup bone and salt in water until meat is tender. Remove from broth, take meat from bone and cut into small pieces. Set meat aside.

Add first four vegetables and cook until tender.

Add remaining ingredients and cook until all vegetables are soft. Stir in meat and serve.

*Makes 12–14 servings*

# Chicken Corn Soup

Chicken and corn have unusually compatible flavors. This soup is a newer twist on the traditional pot pie. With the addition of noodles or rivvels it has a close resemblance to, yet is a welcome variation on, the old favorite. Again, the ingredients are home-grown.

Amish cooks are sought after to prepare the Chicken Corn Soup offered for lunch at local fire company dinners and at the food stands at farm auctions in the Lancaster area.

> 3 – 4 lbs. stewing chicken
> salt to taste
> water
> 2 quarts corn, fresh, frozen or canned
> rivvels (optional)
> 3 – 4 hard-boiled eggs, diced (optional)
> dash of pepper

In large kettle, cover chicken pieces with water. Salt to taste. Cook until tender, then cut meat off bones and dice into bite-sized pieces.

Return chicken to broth. Add corn and bring to a boil. Stir in rivvels or hard-boiled eggs and cook until rivvels are cooked through. Add pepper and serve.

*Makes 8 – 10 servings*

# Ham Soup

Ham Soup is hearty. It was particularly well suited to winter-time eating when meat hung heavily in the attic and the vegetable supply was dwindling.

> 2 – 3 lb. ham
> 1 large onion, minced
> 4 – 5 cups potatoes, peeled and cubed
> large handful of noodles
> 3 quarts milk

Cook ham in water until soft. Cut up and set aside. Cook

potatoes and onions in ham broth until tender.

Meanwhile, cook noodles and drain. Add ham and noodles to potatoes. Add milk and bring to the boiling point. Serve with crackers.

*Makes 12 servings*

# Oyster Stew

Oyster stew brought a special variety to the soup menu in many Amish homes. Those persons who didn't savor the oysters usually claimed to enjoy the flavorful broth! The thin milk base was always given added body with the addition of crackers.

1 quart milk
1 pint stewing oysters
2 Tbsp. butter
1 tsp. salt
dash of pepper

In a 2-quart saucepan heat milk to the boiling point.
In a frying pan melt the butter and brown it.
Drain the oysters; then add them one at a time to the browned butter. Cook for only 2–3 minutes. Add the salt and pepper.
Add the oysters and butter to the hot milk and serve at once.

*Makes 4 servings*

# Cold Soup

The mention of it brings fond smiles to the faces of those over 50 years of age. "My favorite is Cold Soup," an elderly man explained without hesitation. "From strawberry time to the end of peach season you can eat it. Tear up bread—homemade or bought—and put fresh fruit over it with milk.

"We'd have a big meal at noon, then this was a cool treat about 4 o'clock in the afternoon. When we were in the harvest it was a good thing for the men who were more tired than hungry."

The soup was primarily a hot-weather dish, although one grandmother remembers Cold Banana Soup which could be eaten whenever the fruit man came by. By using bread instead of a shortcake, the cook was saved extra baking. The combination may have evolved also as a way to redeem the drier homemade bread common at the turn of the century.

Sometimes Cold Soup was the main meal of the day. Cooked or fried potatoes were frequently served with it to make the meal more substantial.

The cook supplied the ingredients. The persons at the table made their own mixes.

> 1 slice bread
> 1 cup fresh fruit, sliced and sweetened
> 1 cup cold milk

Crumble bread into soup bowl. Dish fruit over top. Sprinkle with sugar if the fruit is not sweetened. Cover with milk ("It's best when the fruit and milk are really cold!").

# Meats

What the meat menu in Amish homes lacked in variety, it made up for in quantity. Historically the German settlers brought with them an expectation of plentiful meat, preferably pork. Many farmers had raised hogs in Germany because the animals did not require a lot of grazing land.[2] Furthermore, these people had learned how to use almost every piece of meat on a pig; head cheese and souse were customarily a part of the butchering task, along with sausage, roasts, ribs and hams.

Hogs were raised in America, as well, but with larger sweeps of pasture land available here, the German settlers also began growing beef cattle. Initially they kept little of it for themselves, sending it instead to the Philadelphia and Baltimore markets.

With the development of the railroads in the 1830s and '40s, competition from large cattle-growers in the Midwest and West undercut the small farmers in the East. The small farmers simply re-focused their market and began selling beef locally and eating it themselves. The Pennsylvania Dutch diet shifted; the Amish and the other German settlers began to eat foods they learned from their English neighbors and others who peopled the Pennsylvania countryside. (One English tradition never entered the Amish menu — mutton. Large-scale sheep-raising did not go well in the heat and humidity of Pennsylvania summers, and the German palate did not seem highly receptive to the flavor of mutton.[3])

Hogs and beef cattle grow well in eastern Pennsylvania. The rich land and accommodating climate have been gifts to those who live here. In turn, the people work hard and they eat well.

One grandmother, born at the opening of the 20th century, has seen change in the amount of meat eaten by the Amish. "My dad used to say that he remembers people figuring you ought to butcher one pig per grown person each winter. We never ate that much. We usually did only two or three hogs totally, and a beef. Already it was tapering off."

Butchering, once a major fall event on nearly every farmstead, is now primarily the domain of commercial butchers who do custom work for neighboring Amish families. Traditionally it was an all-day affair (neighbors and extended family came to help), undertaken before freezing weather since the salt used for curing could not penetrate frozen meat.

"Every corner of the meat was used," smiles one grandmother. The fronts, sides and hindquarters of the hog were smoked; loins and ribs were cut into fresh chops and roasts; large scraps were mixed into sausage (which was, in days gone by, stuffed into cleaned intestinal casings); small scraps were mixed with cornmeal and seasonings into scrapple. The pig's feet were boiled with vinegar and spices to make souse. And finally the excess fat was rendered into lard for cooking and for help in preserving meats. An 80-year-old woman recalls the days before they canned their meat, "We would cook it, then put it in a crock and pour lard over it to seal it. We'd keep it in the cellar so it would stay cool. When it got warmer, we used it up." Another remembers, "We had no refrigeration so we buried pork ribs in fat."

Beef butchering resulted in a similar process. The secondary meat was made into bologna; parts of the hindquarters were smoked and made into dried beef.

Smoking took place in the family smokehouse with abundant care, after the meat was cured (either in a salt brine or in a dry salt cure which was rubbed into the larger cuts). Fired by hickory chips, fruitwood or green stumps, the smokehouse needed the judgment of a veteran to maintain a fire of proper temperature. If it were too hot, the meat would begin to cook; if it were too low a heat, the meat would freeze. In neither case would smoke penetrate as it should.

Depending upon the size of the cuts, smoking took from 24 hours to a week to complete. Experience told when it was time to cover the meat with muslin and move it to the attic.

Liquid smoke is not a new invention. "My parents used liquid smoke," says an 80-year-old. A woman in her 50s, who also remembers its use during her childhood, recalls, "After the smoking we hung the hams in the attic where they dripped grease on the floor if we forgot to put newspaper down! I'll always smell that honey cure."

But few Amish children today will carry such a memory. Says one woman in her early 40s, "My brother-in-law butchers and smokes his own meat, but that's pretty rare. It's been pretty well lost, but it just doesn't pay anymore to take a day off to butcher. Not with large dairies and farms and people being so busy."

A lot of Amish farms still keep a flock of chickens — for laying and for eating. In fact, more chicken is being eaten these days than before. Explains a woman in her mid-50s, "When we wanted to make chicken, Dad would go out and find one that wouldn't lay. But we didn't eat chicken as much then as now."

The flavor of home-cured and home-canned meats is hard to surpass. Yet supermarket cuts rival the cost of custom-butchered meats; food and farm magazines tempt the cook to try new recipes and inform her of health concerns. Here are recipes for the foods eaten when, as one graying man recalled, "Beef and pork were the main meats. We ate some chicken. And sometimes someone would bring home fish."

# Beef Roast

When canning was perfected in the late 19th century, many Amish cooks found that process to be the solution to having meat with a fresh—rather than smoked—flavor, year round. Until then, fresh meat was stored either under fat in the cellar or in the cool springhouse. Recalls one woman, "We had a big water trough in our pantry that was spring-fed. It was as long as a bathtub and we used that to cool food."

Canning took away the pressure to use meat quickly before it spoiled. It provided the cook, too, with the prospect of a nearly instant meal, should drop-in company appear or other duties keep her preoccupied. Many Amish cooks still can meat since they are able to store it at home, in the absence of home freezers.

As important as preparing flavorful and tender meat is creating a good gravy. The cook, whether using fresh or canned meat, intends to have a rich broth to work with when the meat is finished cooking.

> beef roast
> salt and pepper to taste
> water
> flour (use 2½ Tbsp. for each cup of water added after
>     meat is finished roasting)
> water
> salt and pepper to taste

Season roast on all sides with salt and pepper. Place in roast pan and add about ½ inch of water. Cover. Roast at 325°, allowing about 30 minutes per pound if the cut is a high quality (rib roast, for example); about 50–60 minutes per pound if the cut is less tender (a chuck or rump roast, for example).

When meat is tender, remove it from the roasting pan.

Mix or shake flour and additional water together until all lumps are gone. Stir into roast drippings in pan over low heat on top of the stove, until it comes to a boil and thickens slightly into a gravy. Taste and add more salt and pepper if needed.

Slice meat onto platter, pour gravy into boat and serve.

*For roast with bone, allow ⅓ lb. per serving.*
*For boneless roast, allow ¼ lb. per serving.*

# Roast Pork

Follow instructions for roast beef with these exceptions:

Increase roasting temperature to 350°.

For loin cuts, shoulders and picnics allow 35–40 minutes per pound cooking time.

For butts allow 45–50 minutes per pound cooking time.

# Baked Ham

Follow instructions for roast beef with these exceptions:

Do not season with salt and pepper.

Allow the following cooking times:

—a whole ham, uncooked—18–20 minutes per pound.

—a half ham, uncooked—22–25 minutes per pound.

—shoulder or picnic, uncooked—30–35 minutes per pound.

# Spareribs and Sauerkraut

3 lbs. spareribs
salt and pepper
water
1 quart sauerkraut
¼ cup onion, diced (optional)
1 apple, peeled and sliced thin (optional)
3 Tbsp. brown sugar (optional)

Season the meat, then brown slowly in a heavy skillet. Add water to a depth of ½–1 inch. Cover and cook slowly one hour.

Spread sauerkraut over pork. Sprinkle with brown sugar, and onion and apple if desired. Cover and cook slowly one more hour.

*Makes 6 servings*

# Scrapple

Butchering yielded rich meat scraps, too flavorful to give to the animals or simply throw away. Scrapple, however, was not invented in Pennsylvania. It most likely came with settlers from the lower Rhine area of Germany to Philadelphia. So it was in this country that the Amish learned to make the dish.

Two ingredients distinguish the dish — buckwheat and cornmeal (a New World addition), which act as extenders and provide a distinctive flavor.

> 1 lb. pork pudding meat or loose sausage
> 1 quart water or pork broth
> salt and pepper to taste
> 1½ cups cornmeal
> ¼ cup buckwheat flour

Stir pudding meat or loose sausage into 1 quart rapidly boiling water or pork broth.

When the mixture reaches the boiling point slowly add the cornmeal and buckwheat flour. Stir constantly until thickened. Cover and let simmer for 15 minutes over low heat.

Pour into two 1-lb. loaf pans. Cool thoroughly then refrigerate. When scrapple is set, cut in ⅜ to ½ inch slices and fry in hot, greased skillet. When slices are browned and crusty, turn and brown on other side. Serve hot with ketchup, syrup or apple butter.

*Makes 3 – 4 lbs. of scrapple*

# Meat Pudding

Few families do their own butchering these days. Custom butchers have taken over that task and attendant jobs, such as sausage-making and the preparation of meat pudding.

Once a standard breakfast food, "puddin's," as this dish is commonly known, is eaten less frequently today. Its characteristic richness and fattiness once made it beloved, but now makes it suspect for those with nutritional concerns. Many folks still eat it with horseradish or chopped fresh onions over top; others mix catsup with it; some like it spread with apple butter.

A custom butchering firm in eastern Lancaster County provided this recipe in the quantities with which they usually work.

*Make in 500-lb. batches:*

**50% pork liver**
**50% trimmings**
**2 lbs. of salt per hundred pounds of meat**
**6 – 8 ozs. of black pepper per hundred pounds of meat**

Mix ingredients and cook together with water in large iron kettle for 1½ hours. (The iron kettle gives the mixture a browned flavor.)

Drain meat and reserve pork broth. Grind meat. Add broth to it until the finished product has the consistency of barbecued beef.

# Sausage, Smoked and Fresh

Those German immigrants who settled in eastern Pennsylvania did not invent sausage. They developed their taste for the robust meat in Germany, but found it translated well to the New World where they could still grow hogs and do their own butchering.

Sausage was, and is, eaten both smoked and fresh. The fresh variety was either cooked and canned for future use or buried under fat in crocks kept in the cool cellar for more immediate use.

Smoked sausage, after being smoked, hung in the attic, offering its spicy flavor throughout the winter.

Both varieties were commonly prepared by browning the pieces and serving them with potatoes.

> 1½ lbs. sausage, fresh or smoked
> ½ cup water
> 2 – 3 Tbsp. flour
> 2 – 3 cups water

Cut sausage in 4-inch lengths. Brown well on all sides in skillet. Add ½ cup water, cover and cook for 15 – 20 minutes or until sausage is fully cooked.

Remove sausage from pan and keep warm.

Mix or shake flour and 2 – 3 cups water together until all lumps are gone. Stir into sausage drippings in pan over low heat until it comes to a boil and thickens slightly into a gravy.

Return sausage to pan and heat thoroughly. Serve.

*Makes 4 – 6 servings*

# Dried Beef Gravy

Twenty-pound slabs of fresh beef were regularly dried at butchering time. The dry salt curing, followed by smoking, and finally, the meat's hanging undisturbed for six weeks, resulted in a pungently strong beef for sandwiches and dried beef gravy. Traditionally the meat was chipped off the chunk in thin slices.

> 4 Tbsp. butter or margarine
> ¼ lb. dried beef, thinly sliced

4 Tbsp. flour
2½ cups milk

Melt butter in skillet. Tear dried beef into shreds and drop into the butter. Stir to coat with butter and then let cook until beef browns around the edges.

Dust beef with flour. Let that mixture brown. Add milk gradually, stirring continuously, while cooking over low heat.

Cook until gravy has thickened and is smooth.

*Makes 4 – 6 servings*

*Note*: Water may be used instead of milk if a lighter broth is desired.

# Roast Chicken

4 – 5 lb. hen
salt and pepper
bread filling (see page 112)
melted butter or margarine
½ cup water

Rub inside of hen with salt. Sprinkle with pepper. Stuff bird lightly with filling. Close opening with skewers and laced string.

Rub outside of stuffed chicken with melted shortening. Salt and pepper, then place in roasting pan. Add water. Baste with drippings every 20 minutes.

Bake at 350° allowing 30 minutes per pound. Test for doneness by twisting drumstick to see if it moves easily or by inserting fork in fleshy part of thigh. If the juice runs clear, chicken should be done.

Serve with giblet gravy (see page 52).

*Makes 8 – 10 servings*

# Roast Turkey

Follow the same procedure for roast chicken (page 51) with these changes:

Bake at 325°.

For a turkey under 12 lbs., allow 30–45 minutes per pound (the longer time for a smaller turkey). For a turkey over 12 lbs., allow 20–30 minutes per pound.

# Giblet Gravy

Cover heart, neck and gizzard from chicken or turkey in salt water, bring to a boil and cook until tender, about 1 hour. Add liver and cook an additional 10 minutes.

Lift meat from broth and cool. Cut into small pieces and set aside. Pour broth into bowl and set aside.

Melt 4 Tbsp. butter or margarine (or equivalent amount of drippings from chicken or turkey roasting pan) in pan where giblets were cooked. Add 1 Tbsp. flour for each cup of reserved broth. Brown flour slightly.

Stir in reserved broth over low heat, stirring constantly until gravy is smooth and thickened. Add giblets to gravy and warm. Serve over mashed potatoes and filling.

# Baked, Creamed Chicken

Because a flock of chickens had the run of most farmsteads, fresh chicken was nearly always a possibility. The efficient cook, on the other hand, preferred to gear up a butchering operation for more than just one fowl. Periodically, a day for doing chicken was, and is, set aside. Those birds that have reached optimum maturity are killed, plucked, dressed and preserved (either canned or frozen, depending upon how accessible a frozen food locker or neighbor's freezer is).

1 chicken, cut up in serving pieces
½ cup flour
1 tsp. salt

dash of pepper
3 Tbsp. butter or margarine
1½ cups cream

Mix flour, salt and pepper together. Dredge chicken in mixture.

Melt butter or margarine in skillet. Brown floured chicken on both sides, then place in roasting pan. Pour cream over chicken. Cover.

Bake at 350° for 1½–2 hours.

*Makes 6 servings*

# Baked Fried Chicken

1 chicken, cut up
1 egg, beaten
½ cup milk
1 tsp. salt
dash of pepper
¾–1 cup cracker crumbs
4 Tbsp. butter or margarine

Mix beaten egg and milk together. Dip chicken in liquid.

Stir together salt, pepper and cracker crumbs. Dip chicken in dry mixture, using spoon to cover chicken well.

Melt butter or margarine in skillet. Brown breaded chicken well on both sides.

Remove browned pieces to roaster. Cover and bake at 325° for 30 minutes. Uncover and continue baking for an additional 30 minutes.

*Makes 6 servings*

# Turkey Stuffed with Duck

One imaginative Amish woman with a large family to feed found a way to avoid the risk of serving a dry turkey to her brood. "I stuff a duck inside a turkey. That makes the turkey more moist and the duck seem less greasy. They both brown well and you can mix the two meats when you serve them!"

> 25 lb. turkey
> 3 lb. duck
> filling (see page 112)
> butter
> salt

Stuff the duck inside the turkey, or lay the duck beside the turkey in the roast pan if using a smaller turkey. Stuff both the duck and turkey with filling.

Rub the turkey with butter and salt. Add water to a depth of ½–1 inch. Cover and bake at 350° allowing 20 minutes per pound, combined weight.

# Fried Oysters

Oysters were a regular treat on the Amish menu. Eastern Pennsylvania's proximity to the Chesapeake Bay brought the delicacy within easy reach of the cooks of the area. Folks today remember two primary ways they got oysters. A woman in her mid-30s said, "Some man from Philadelphia came up regularly with oysters and fruit. Mom would ask for 50-cents worth of bananas and that was really a lot. Then she'd buy oysters to fry, scallop or put in soup."

Another woman, in her 80s, recalls that neighbors would buy a barrel of oysters, dump them out on the floor of their tobacco shed, cover them with damp feed bags to keep them cool, then sell them to anyone who wanted them.

> 3 dozen frying oysters
> ½ tsp. salt
> ½ cup cracker crumbs, finely crushed

1 egg, beaten
2 Tbsp. water
butter or margarine

Drain oysters. Meanwhile combine salt and crumbs. Dip oysters in crumbs. Combine egg and water. Dip oysters in that liquid. Dip again in crumbs, using spoon to coat thoroughly.

Melt butter in skillet. Fry oysters, turning so that both sides brown evenly.

*Makes 8 – 10 servings*

# Scalloped Oysters

4 cups crackers, coarsely crushed
1 pint medium-sized oysters
2 cups milk
1 egg
1 tsp. salt
pepper to taste
⅓ cup butter or margarine

Line 1½-quart casserole with half of the crackers. Place half of the oysters on crushed crackers. Layer remaining crackers on top of oysters followed by the rest of the oysters.

Beat egg and add milk, salt and pepper to it.

Just before baking pour mixture over oysters and crackers. Arrange butter in thin slices on top.

Bake at 375° for 30 minutes.

*Makes 4 – 5 servings*

# Souse
## (Pickled Pigs' Feet)

The German immigrants to Pennsylvania brought with them the understanding that an acidic food could offset the richness of many of their meats and main dishes. Coupled with that was their zest for using everything and wasting nothing. Pickled pigs' feet, commonly known as "souse," fulfilled both intents.

    4 pigs' feet
    2 cups stock
    2 cups apple vinegar
    2 Tbsp. salt
    ½ tsp. pepper
    1 Tbsp. whole cloves
    1 cinnamon stick
    1 cup sweet pickles, chopped

Clean feet, scraping them well. Place in deep kettle and cover with salt water.

Bring to boil, then simmer for about 4 hours or until meat comes easily off the bone. Cut meat in small pieces and set aside.

Mix together 2 cups cooking stock, vinegar, seasonings and spices. Bring to boil and continue boiling for 30 minutes.

Strain out spices. Lay chopped meat and pickles in bottom of loaf pan. Pour boiled liquid over it. Chill completely until mixture congeals and is thoroughly set. Slice and serve as a salad, side dish or snack.

# Vegetables

Spring without a garden in the Amish community is as inconceivable as a Lancaster Amish wedding without creamed celery! Here, home-grown vegetables are an assumed part of life. The Amish cook's calendar revolves around the times for planting and harvesting vegetables and fruits.

These people are dependent upon the land; the seasons mark their activities. Not only does the Amish farmer bear responsibility for plowing the fields; he is also expected to turn over the earth in the garden, "working it fine," as soon in the spring as the threat of frost is passed.

The Amish demonstrate many of their principles in their gardens. There they display their respect for life; they are stewards of the earth. The people are blessed, in this part of the world, with rich soil and a balanced mix of humidity, sun and rainfall. To that they add their willingness to work hard, as well as the knowledge they have accumulated by having many generations living from the earth.

The garden is the site of inter-generational tutelage. Here grandparents and parents teach their children the care of the land. The children learn persistence, tedium and reward.

Gardening is a major family industry. Large families with growing children, many of whom exercise vigorously with their farm chores, require a lot of food. The cook's task is to plant plenty, then manage the weeds, the picking, the daily preparation of what has matured, as well as the preservation of the abundance so that the food supply lasts until the next summer's bounty is ready.

Peas and onions go in early—during mid-March if the weather cooperates. The faithful perennials—asparagus, dandelion, strawberries, rhubarb—begin to appear in May. Planting continues in earnest with the full weight of the garden's productivity coming in June, July and August. It is a time of nearly too much work, too much food, too relentless a sun.

The payoff, of course, is in the late summer basement—floor-to-ceiling canning shelves loaded with preserved vegetables and fruits—and in the family's frozen food locker (several local grocery stores provide this rented service for the Amish who do not have large home freezers because they choose not to use electricity from public utilities).

Meanwhile, during the summer months everyone has grown accustomed to feasting on fresh vegetables that have ripened on the vine and have not been shipped from anywhere.

According to this food tradition, only raw vegetables are meant to be crispy and crunchy; cooked vegetables are best if they are cooked soft! Green peas and sugar peas, string beans and lima beans, carrots, asparagus, cabbage and cauliflower are usually served salted and covered with brown butter. A cheese or cream sauce may accompany them. But, in general, vegetables are prepared simply. They are regularly part of the main meal of the day. Potatoes, that basic Amish food, are likely to appear at breakfast, dinner and supper, and are even mixed into buns and doughnuts (page 106)!

# Baked Corn

Corn, fresh or canned, can be made into a pleasing custard. Eggs and milk are still plentiful on most Amish homesteads.

2 cups corn
2 eggs
1 cup milk
1 Tbsp. flour
1 Tbsp. sugar, optional
½ tsp. salt
dash of pepper
2 Tbsp. melted butter or margarine
½ cup bread or cracker crumbs
2 Tbsp. butter or margarine

Cook the corn. Beat the eggs and milk. Combine corn, eggs and milk, seasonings and 2 Tbsp. butter or margarine. Mix well.

Pour into greased 1½-quart baking dish. Mix crumbs and butter and sprinkle over corn. Bake at 350° for 40 minutes or until mixture is set.

*Makes 6 servings*

# Corn Fritters

"We used to eat a lot of corn fritters near the end of the corn season when it was beginning to get old. We would grate it so it was creamy."

Corn is a favorite vegetable among these people, relished in its many forms — corn on the cob, creamed corn, corn fritters, dried corn, chicken corn soup, and more.

Corn fritters are of two main varieties — doughy little balls, laced with corn, that are deep-fried; and the pancake type that are made of more corn than batter and browned in a skillet. Family tradition usually determines which kind are served. Nutrition would nod in favor of the pancake variety, described below.

> 2 cups fresh, grated corn
> 2 eggs, beaten
> ¾ cup flour
> ¾ tsp. salt
> ¼ tsp. pepper
> 1 tsp. baking powder

Combine corn and eggs. Add flour which has been sifted with remaining ingredients.

Drop corn mixture from tablespoon into 1 inch of melted shortening. Brown until golden on both sides, turning once.

*Makes 12 fritters*

# Cooked Dried Corn

*Field* corn is roasted for grinding into cornmeal flour. *Sweet* corn is dried and then eaten as a hot vegetable. When the sweet corn season had passed, this dish was prepared. Today, dried sweet corn is produced commercially in Lancaster County for those who no longer dry their own.

> 2 cups dried sweet corn
> warm water
> 1 tsp. salt
> 2 tsp. sugar

½ cup cream or sweet milk

Soak corn for 1 hour in warm water that nearly covers the corn. Then cook corn until it is soft and the water is almost completely absorbed.

Stir in salt, sugar and cream or milk and bring to a boil. Serve.

*Makes 6 – 8 servings*

# Corn Pie

Here, corn in combination with potatoes makes a meal. Add chicken chunks and you have an adaptation of chicken pot pie.

Pastry for a 2-crust pie
3 cups fresh corn
1½ cups raw potatoes, diced
2 or 3 hard-boiled eggs, diced
salt and pepper to taste
2 Tbsp. flour
milk

Line a casserole or deep pie pan with pastry.

Combine corn, potatoes and eggs and pour into pastry-lined container. Add salt and pepper. Sprinkle with flour. Add enough milk to cover the vegetables.

Cover with top pastry. Pinch edges together to seal.

Bake at 425° for 30 – 40 minutes, until crust is browned and milk is bubbly throughout.

*Variation:*

Add chunks of chicken cut into 1″ pieces.

# Baked Beans

Navy beans (the "Lazy Wife" variety, see page 36) and lima beans grew in the garden or along the cornfields. Many were dried for wintertime use. As one grandmother remarked, "Baked beans are an old dish. We had no freezer and so they were a good substitute for fresh vegetables."

> 1 lb. dried navy beans
> one small onion, minced
> 8 slices of bacon or 1 cup ham, cut up
> 1½ tsp. salt
> ¼ tsp. pepper
> ½ cup brown sugar
> 2 cups tomato juice
> ½ – 1 cup water from cooking beans, if needed

Soak beans overnight (8 cups water to 2 cups of beans). Cook 2–3 hours in soaking water until beans are nearly soft. Drain (save water for cooking other vegetables, since it has nutrients from the beans).
Add rest of ingredients to drained beans.
Bake at 325° for 2–3 hours. If mixture becomes dry, stir in ½–1 cup soaking water.

*Makes 8–10 servings*

# Tomato Gravy

Tomatoes last into cornhusking time in the fall. One Amish grandmother has warm memories of both her mother and grandmother fixing tomato gravy to ladle over fried potatoes. It was their welcome for those who had spent cool fall evenings in the fields.

> 1 quart peeled tomato slices or canned tomatoes
> 3 Tbsp. flour
> 2–3 Tbsp. water
> 4 Tbsp. brown sugar

Heat tomatoes slowly until they reach the boiling point.

Meanwhile, stir flour and water together until smooth.

When tomatoes come to a boil, add flour-water paste and sugar, stirring until the gravy thickens. Eat over fried potatoes or toast.

*Makes 6 servings*

# Fried Tomato Slices

For a small table-full of eaters (this requires a lot of hustling for the cook)!

3 firm, almost ripe tomatoes
1 egg beaten
2 Tbsp. milk
1 cup cracker crumbs
¼ cup lard, butter or margarine
salt and pepper to taste

Slice tomatoes into ¾″ slices.

Combine egg and milk. Dip each tomato slice in egg mixture and then into cracker crumbs.

Melt shortening and fry coated tomato slices. Brown on both sides, turning once. Season with salt and pepper.

*Makes 6 – 8 servings*

# Fried Tomato Gravy

For a hungry crowd (this allows the cook time to get the potatoes mashed)!

3 ripened tomatoes
¼ – ⅓ cup flour
4 Tbsp. butter or margarine, melted
2 Tbsp. brown sugar
2½ cups milk

Slice tomatoes. Dip in flour. Fry in butter and margarine. When thickened, stir in brown sugar and gradually add milk. Cook over low heat until thickened, stirring constantly. Keep warm until ready to eat.

*Makes 6 servings*

# Fried Potatoes

**6 medium-sized potatoes**
**3 Tbsp. lard, butter or margarine**
**1 tsp. salt**
**dash of pepper**
**2 eggs, beaten**

Cook potatoes until soft. Cool and skin.

Melt shortening. Slice potatoes and slide into skillet. Pour beaten eggs over and season.

Let potatoes brown until crispy edges form. Then turn over with metal spatula, allowing other edges to brown.

*Makes 6 servings*

*Variation:*

Use only 4 or 5 potatoes. Begin by toasting 2 buttered slices of bread, torn in bite-sized pieces, in hot skillet. Then add potatoes and continue as above.

# Riced Mashed Potatoes

It was in the 1770s that Europeans first ate potatoes in major quantities. Only when bad growing seasons hit their grain crops did the people eat what they earlier regarded as a lower-class food.

The Hessian fly threatened the wheat crop on American farms from 1770–1800. Potatoes did not replace breads and noodles for the German settlers, but they did become a substantial supplement to their diets from then on. By the mid-19th century, potatoes were frequently on the menu three times a day.

Amish families still eat a lot of potatoes — they like their flavor, and they find them substantial. Eaten alongside schnitz pie, they make a more serious meal of an otherwise quickie snack. Mashed or riced potatoes give strength to nearly any menu. Potatoes at breakfast time last well until lunch.

New potato recipes continue to be invented. Here are a few old favorites that have survived through the generations.

**6 medium-sized potatoes, peeled and cut in chunks**

Sauerkraut-Making (pages 68-69)

Old-Fashioned Crumb Cake with Fresh Strawberries (page 141)

½ – ¾ cup milk, scalded
½ tsp. salt
brown butter

Cook potatoes until very soft in small amount of water. Pour ½ cup milk and salt into the saucepan with the potatoes.

With a manual potato ricer, immediately mash the potatoes by hand. Add additional milk if they seem too stiff.

Stop mashing at whichever stage you prefer — when the potatoes have been formed into noodle-like strands, or when they are as smooth as an electric mixer's end result. (The Amish, because they do not have electricity in their homes, always mash their potatoes by hand.)

Cover with brown butter.

*Makes 6 servings*

# Potato Cakes

Leftover mashed potatoes never go to waste. In fact, some family members wish there were more of them — more often — so that potato cakes were prepared more frequently.

Potato cakes are at their best if they are eaten immediately after leaving the frying pan.

2 cups leftover mashed potatoes
1 egg, beaten
1 Tbsp. flour, or more if the potatoes are thin
2 Tbsp. cream, or less if the potatoes are thin
1 Tbsp. onion, chopped fine
2 – 3 Tbsp. shortening

Mix together all ingredients except shortening. Heat shortening. Drop potatoes by tablespoons into shortening and brown on both sides.

*Makes 4 – 6 servings*

# Creamed Potatoes

6 – 8 medium-sized potatoes
salt
2 Tbsp. butter or margarine
2 Tbsp. flour
½ tsp. salt
dash of pepper
2 cups milk
¾ cup cheese, grated (optional)

Peel and dice potatoes. Cook until soft in water, slightly salted. Drain until nearly dry.

While potatoes cook, melt butter or margarine. Stir in flour and seasonings to form paste. Gradually add milk, over heat, stirring constantly. When sauce comes to boil, cook for 1 minute until it is smooth and thickened.

Add cheese, if desired, stirring until it melts.

Fold sauce into cooked potatoes and serve.

*Makes 6 – 8 servings*

# New Potatoes and Peas

This is a springtime feast. Some cooks favor only a brown butter dressing; others prefer a white sauce.

New potatoes may be cooked in their papery skins, or they may be gently scraped with a knife (not a potato peeler) so that only the thin shell is removed.

12 small new potatoes
3 cups fresh peas
1 tsp. salt
brown butter or a white sauce

Cook potatoes in a small amount of water until almost soft. Add peas and cook just until they and the potatoes are tender. Salt.

Spoon into serving dish and pour brown butter or white sauce over.

*Makes 4 – 6 servings*

*White Sauce*

**2 Tbsp. butter or margarine**
**1½ tsp. flour**
**1½ cups milk**

Melt butter or margarine. Stir in flour to form paste. Gradually add milk, stirring constantly over heat until smooth and thickened.

# Candied Sweet Potatoes

Sweet potatoes have traditionally had two steps to their preparation and eating. One evening the whole sweet potatoes were steamed in their jackets, then eaten for supper, spread with butter and sprinkled with salt. The cooked potatoes that were not eaten (a large batch was prepared so a meal's-worth would be left) were fried for the next day's dinner or supper.

**6 medium sweet potatoes, cooked**
**salt**
**¼ cup butter or margarine**
**¾ cup brown sugar**
**½ – ¾ cup water**

Remove peels from cooked sweet potatoes. Cut potatoes in half lengthwise.

Melt the butter or margarine in a frying pan. Add sugar and stir until it melts. Add water and bring to a boil.

Lay sweet potato slices in syrup and cook slowly, using metal spatula to turn slices so both sides brown evenly.

*Makes 6 servings*

# Making Sauerkraut

The Amish worked out their vegetable supply to last the year around, as did many other early settlers in the days before canning was perfected and freezing was possible. Cabbages, heads of cauliflower, carrots and beets could be buried underground for the winter and kept from freezing by insulating the hole with leaves and straw, then covering it with layers of boards and dirt. The root cellar of the farmhouse held the potatoes, onions and apples.

Sauerkraut developed as a way to preserve cabbage. It was a dish the German settlers learned in Europe, but it was compatible with the seasonal cycle of the New World also. Once seen as a peasant dish eaten only by "backward" farmers, sauerkraut, by the beginning of the 20th century, was enjoyed throughout the country and by all strata of society.

Although a common Amish dish, sauerkraut was not made by all Amish families, nor eaten by all. The old method of shredding it into a large crock, salting each layer, stomping it down firmly to break the strong fibers and release the natural juices, then weighting the top of the full crock heavily so the fermentation could preserve it for the winter is now a memory of the older members of the community. Today few cooks use only that method. Some may follow the process to a point, but as a final step, can the sauerkraut. A woman in her mid-50s explains, "We let the cabbage ferment in the crock for about ten days, depending on how warm the weather is. Then we cold-pack it in jars. That way we don't have a lot of spoilage as we used to, and we don't have to use it as fast." (The cabbage at the top of the crock blackened on contact with the air. The cook needed to lift that off and use the sauerkraut before the spoilage spread into the depths of the crock.)

Shred cabbage into narrow strips, about ⅛″ wide. Add 3 Tbsp. salt to about 5 pounds of cabbage. Mix well. Pack tightly into clean quart jars. Fill with boiling water (to within ½ inch of the top of each jar). Turn lids on loosely and let jar stand in a dishpan for about 10 days (the fermentation process causes the juice to expand and run over the edge of the jars). Turn the lids on tightly and store. The sauerkraut is ready to use immediately.

*Variation:*
After filling the jars with boiling water, seal them tightly immediately. Set in dish pan because the fermenting will cause the juice to expand and squeeze out of the jars. Let set for 4 to 6 weeks before using.

When ready to use, pour into pan and heat or pile around pork roast or spareribs and bake.

# Sweet and Sour Steamed Cabbage

"My mother used to add sour cream to cooked cabbage. Then we'd have a little container of vinegar on the table and we'd pour some over the cabbage on our plates." It's a practice the 80-year-old woman still keeps. "We cut the cabbage in chunks, steam it tender, then eat it with a little pickle juice or vinegar and sugar added. You feel better that way," she states with sureness.

    1 medium-sized head of cabbage
    1 tsp. salt
    2 Tbsp. butter or margarine
    3 Tbsp. sugar
    3 Tbsp. vinegar

Cut cabbage in narrow wedges and steam in small amount of water until tender. Stir in butter.

Combine sugar and vinegar. Pour over cabbage and heat thoroughly.

*Makes 6 – 8 servings*

# Warm Slaw

A variation on sweet and sour cabbage, warm slaw has a creamier dressing but a similar effect.

 2 Tbsp. butter
 1 quart shredded cabbage
 1 tsp. salt
 1½ cups water
 5 Tbsp. sugar
 1 egg, beaten
 1 Tbsp. flour
 ½ cup milk
 2 Tbsp. vinegar

Melt butter in saucepan and add cabbage. Stir thoroughly; then add salt and water. Cover and cook 10 minutes.

In a bowl mix sugar, egg, flour and milk. Add to the cabbage. Cook another minute. Add the vinegar and serve.

*Makes 4 servings*

# Peas with Knepp

"Schnitz and knepp," a ham-apple-dumpling dish usually attributed to the Pennsylvania Dutch food tradition, is not commonly eaten by the Amish of Lancaster County. Nor do they remember it ever being a part of their family diet. "We'd eat peas and knepp, but *not* schnitz and knepp. That seems to be a Lutheran and Reformed dish," smiled one Amish historian, referring to Germanic peoples of a different faith community. "Our knepp are fluffy," he added.

 1½ cups flour
 2 tsp. baking powder
 ¾ tsp. salt
 3 Tbsp. shortening
 ¾ cup milk
 6 cups fresh peas
 brown butter

Combine flour, baking powder and salt. Cut in shortening. Blend in milk.

Place peas in large kettle and add enough water to cover peas. Cook about 10 minutes.

Drop knepp dough by spoonfuls on top of boiling peas. Cook slowly for 10 minutes, uncovered. Cover with dome lid and cook 10 minutes longer. Serve drizzled with brown butter.

*Makes 10 – 12 servings*

# Creamed Asparagus

Some folks delight in the full flavor of spring's first asparagus —they want it simply steamed and drizzled with brown butter.

Others prefer it dressed up a little. Sometimes the presence of toast and eggs help children learn to eat a vegetable that is less familiar since it comes only seasonally to the table.

**asparagus spears**
**butter or margarine**
**flour**
**salt**
**pepper**
**toast**
**hard-boiled eggs**

Steam asparagus in ½ inch of water until soft. Lift out of water and set aside, keeping it warm.

To 1 cup of cooking water add 2 Tbsp. butter or margarine, 2 Tbsp. flour, ¼ tsp. salt, dash of pepper. Stir until smooth and thickened.

Place asparagus in serving dish. Put squares of toast around the edge and slices of hard-boiled eggs on top. Pour cream sauce over and serve.

*Note:* This cream sauce, usually without the addition of toast and hard-boiled eggs, is frequently prepared with peas and green beans.

# Creamed Celery

Creamed celery is traditionally prepared for the feast which follows a wedding in the Lancaster Amish community. Most weddings occur in November and December, so celery is one of the few fresh vegetables available then. Since it is not usually raised in quantity, it is not eaten routinely for main daily meals. Creamed celery, then, is a delicacy adding to the celebration.

It is the custom for a family with a daughter planning to be married in the fall to put out an unusually large celery patch. Alert neighbors and visitors learn from that cue that a wedding will be coming up! The formal announcement of the event takes place only a week or two before the wedding itself.

One mother of nine, who has made an abundance of creamed celery, explains that vinegar is added to prevent the cream sauce from curdling. The sweet-sour dressing is present here again, another example of that particular taste preference among the Amish.

> 12 quarts celery, cut up in chunks
> 2 cups water
> 1¼ cups granulated sugar
> 4 Tbsp. butter or margarine
> 2 Tbsp. salt
> ¼ cup vinegar
> 3 Tbsp. flour
> 1 cup brown sugar
> 1½ cups cream

Cook celery with water, granulated sugar, butter or margarine and salt until soft.

Mix together vinegar, flour, brown sugar and cream until smooth. Stir into cooked celery and continue heating until well blended.

# Cooked Rice

Sometimes the line between dessert and main course is blurry. Take the old tradition of sweetening certain vegetables, for example. Although the Amish generally prefer mild seasonings, they seem to find some dishes too bland without the help of added flavoring: the older people, especially, like some sugar with their rice when they eat it as a vegetable.

Perhaps the Amish first enjoyed rice as a pudding before immigrating to America. The old dish was eaten in Germany in the 16th century. Whatever their first acquaintance with rice, many Amish have always preferred it with sugar, simply adding more if the rice is served for dessert.

"When my mother made rice as a vegetable, she always made extra so she could have enough for dessert. She made it a little sweet as a vegetable, but she'd add whipped cream and pineapples to it for a dessert."

Particular combinations, varying from family to family, were traditionally eaten with rice. One woman in her late 50s explains, "We'd often eat tomato sauce over rice as a vegetable." Remembers another, "We used to have cooked rice with milk and sugar added to it with cinnamon on top. That was served hot with raw-fried potatoes."

1¼ cups water
1¼ cups milk
1 cup rice
½ tsp. salt
2 – 3 tsp. sugar
1 Tbsp. butter or margarine

Mix water and milk in a saucepan and bring to a boil. Stir in remaining ingredients. Cover tightly, allowing mixture to simmer for 20 minutes, or until tender and liquid is absorbed.

*Makes 5 – 6 servings*

# Fried Eggplant

This vegetable is eaten only seasonally and then not regularly. Perhaps it is simply impractical to prepare such a last-minute, labor-intensive dish for a large, hungry family.

1 eggplant, peeled and cut into ½″ slices
2 eggs
⅓ cup milk
cracker crumbs
butter or margarine

Combine eggs and milk. Dip slices into liquid, then into cracker crumbs.

Fry slowly in butter or margarine, turning to brown evenly on both sides.

# Fried Oyster Plant

Salsify, because of its faint oyster flavor, is commonly known as "oyster plant." It flourishes in eastern Pennsylvania gardens.

One grandmother, who recalls that they "always had it in the garden," explained that salsify makes good soup, also. "We sliced it like a carrot, cooked it soft, and added butter, salt, pepper and milk."

oyster plant
salt
egg, beaten
cracker crumbs
butter or margarine

Scrub oyster plant. Steam in water to which ½ tsp. salt has been added.

When soft, slice it and dip individual slices in egg, then in cracker crumbs.

Fry in butter or margarine, turning to brown evenly on both sides.

# Salads and Greens

Salads, of the leafy green variety, were on the menu in most Amish homes primarily at one particular time of the year — in the early springtime. It was then that the root cellar was growing increasingly bare; fresh vegetables from the garden were still being awaited.

These people of the land celebrated the coming of spring by foraging for young dandelion shoots and eating watercress sandwiches. Those practices, of course, were shared by others who lived off the land, especially when shipped foods were either not available or not desirable.

When fresh greens were out of season, the Amish supplemented their meat-and-potatoes mainstays with applesauce and pickled relishes, or cooked salads such as potato and macaroni with sweet-and-sour dressings.

Amish cooks concur that in this area, also, change is apparent. An elderly woman commented, "We always ate dandelion in the spring. Now we've started eating lettuce. It's easier — and better." Her daughter reflected further, "Around here you have to watch for sprayed grass. I'm afraid eating wild-growing dandelion is a thing of the past."

"There are still some people who like their applesauce. But I know today we eat more tossed salads," offered a woman in her early 40s. A woman ten years younger agreed, "Applesauce used to be eaten three times a day. I seldom serve it more than once a day. I know that there are a lot more tossed salads eaten today among the Amish than there used to be." This is especially true among the younger people.

The Amish sweet tooth has been captured by the multitude of gelatin-based salads popular today. Cooks find those recipes on food packages and in farm magazines (rather than in their mother's hand-written notes!); they share them with each other at sisters' days and at school picnics.

The old seasonal salads may be fading, but they haven't been replaced. Most cooks can light up the eaters at their tables by serving bowls of fresh cutting lettuce! Here, then, are favorites from years past that are still considered treats today.

# Fresh Cutting Lettuce

The first taste of spring!

1½ quarts cutting lettuce (oakleaf or black-seeded
    simpson are especially good!)
¾ cup cream
2 Tbsp. sugar
2 Tbsp. vinegar
3 hard-boiled eggs, diced

Fill a 1½-quart serving dish heaping full of washed, drained lettuce. Set aside.

Stir together cream and sugar. Add vinegar 1 tsp. at a time until dressing is creamy and thick.

Pour over lettuce and eggs and serve.

*Makes 6 servings*

# Watercress Sandwiches

Watercress grows bountifully and without cultivation along fresh water streams in the springtime. Farm families cut it primarily to eat in sandwiches rather than in salads where its tangy flavor can predominate.

handful of watercress, washed
2 slices of bread
butter or margarine

Pat watercress dry. Pile onto buttered bread, cover with top slice and eat.

# Dandelion Salad
# (or Endive or Spinach Salad)

The best eyes in the family are needed to spot the earliest shoots of dandelion in the spring. If the stalks have blossoms, the leaves are already too bitter to eat.

Endive and spinach may be substituted for dandelion with equally good results.

> **1 quart young dandelion greens**
> **3 eggs, hard-boiled (optional)**

Cut fine-leafed, young dandelion leaves and stalks in early spring. Wash carefully, then chop or tear into 1″ long pieces. Top with sliced eggs.

Cover with hot bacon dressing and serve.

*Variation:*

Some folks want to be sure their dandelion is wilted before eating (covering the greens with a hot dressing only partially accomplishes that). The following procedure assures that result.

Pull the dandelion leaves off their stalks and chop the leaves. Drop them in a pot of boiling water. Let stand for 5 – 10 minutes. Then drain leaves, pouring off juice.

# Hot Bacon Dressing

Many less-than-enthusiastic dandelion eaters agree that the best thing about dandelion salad is the hot bacon dressing traditionally served over it!

The dressing reflects the ingredients commonly available on Amish farms in eastern Pennsylvania. Most homesteads had at least a cow or two for their own dairy supplies and usually also had a flock of chickens. Bacon and lard came by way of butchering; vinegar was often home-produced from the abundantly fruitful apple trees on the property.

Furthermore the blend of flavors is sweet and sour, that specialty of these people who like its taste and digestive properties.

Many variations on this dressing have developed; some use no bacon, fat or egg and are served cold (often over cole slaw); others use spices (occasionally dry mustard); still others call for chopped onion.

4 strips bacon
½ cup sugar
2 Tbsp. flour
1 egg, beaten
1 tsp. salt
½ cup vinegar
1½ cups water

Brown bacon; remove from drippings and crumble.

Combine sugar and flour. Add egg, salt, vinegar and water and mix until smooth. Pour into bacon drippings and heat, stirring constantly, until mixture thickens. Add crumbled bacon.

*Makes 2 cups*

# Homemade Salad Dressing

¾ cup oil
1 egg
1½ tsp. prepared mustard
2 tsp. salt
⅓ cup sugar
½ cup plus 2½ Tbsp. flour
⅓ cup sugar
⅓ cup vinegar
1 cup water

Mix thoroughly the oil, egg, mustard, salt and ⅓ cup sugar. Set aside. Over low heat blend flour, ⅓ cup sugar, vinegar and water. Bring to boil, stirring constantly until thickened. Combine well with first mixture.

*Makes 3 cups*

# Cole Slaw

Cole slaw comes primarily in two forms—with a creamy sweet-sour dressing in which the vinegar is somewhat underplayed, and with a sharper dressing in which no milk product is used and the vinegar flavor is predominant. Each cook's balance of ingredients is her own. The interplay between sweet and sour varies from household to household and is only subtly sensed by an outsider to the community, but is known well by those within!

**3 cups cabbage, shredded**

*Variation:*
Shred one small carrot and chop ½ of a green pepper. Blend with cabbage to add flavor and color.

*Dressing 1*

**⅓ cup sweet or sour cream**
**2 Tbsp. granulated sugar**
**2 Tbsp. apple cider vinegar**
**½ tsp. salt**

Mix together dressing ingredients until smooth. Fold into shredded cabbage. Cool and serve.

*Makes 6 servings*

*Dressing 2*

**¾ cup granulated sugar**
**¼ cup vinegar**
**½ tsp. salt**
**2 Tbsp. water**

Mix together until smooth. Fold into shredded cabbage. Cool and serve.

# Cucumbers and Onions

2 medium cucumbers
2 medium onions
salt
2–3 Tbsp. mayonnaise or salad dressing (see page 79)
1 Tbsp. sugar
1 Tbsp. vinegar

Peel cucumbers and slice thin. Layer in shallow dish, sprinkling each layer with salt. Let stand overnight.

In the morning, drain cucumbers and rinse. Let dry on paper towels.

Slice onions thin. Mix gently with cucumber slices.

Beat together the mayonnaise or salad dressing, sugar and vinegar until creamy. Stir into mixed cucumbers and onions. (The dressing should be plentiful so the salad is creamy. Increase amounts of dressing ingredients, proportionally, if needed.)

*Makes 4–6 servings*

# Potato Salad

The cooked, thickened dressings traditionally favored by the Pennsylvania Germans are eaten widely today, especially on potato and macaroni salads. It is likely that these dishes, especially potato salad, filled the vegetable gap that developed near the end of the winter and before the garden was producing. All necessary ingredients were present, even at that time of the year. If the chickens weren't laying well, eggs could be eliminated from the salad itself; flour could be used in their place in the dressing.

6 medium-sized potatoes
1 small onion, chopped fine
1 cup celery, chopped
1 tsp. celery seed
1 tsp. salt
4 hard-cooked eggs, diced

Cook potatoes in their jackets until soft. Peel and dice.
Mix potatoes gently with the remaining five ingredients. Pour dressing over and stir.

*Dressing*

2 eggs, well beaten
3/4 cup sugar
1 tsp. cornstarch
salt to taste
1/4 – 1/2 cup vinegar
1/2 cup cream
1 tsp. mustard
3 Tbsp. butter, softened
1 cup salad dressing (see page 79)

Mix eggs with sugar, cornstarch and salt. Add vinegar, cream and mustard. Cook until thickened.
Remove from heat and beat in butter. Add salad dressing and mix until smooth.
Fold into potato mixture.

*Makes 10 servings*

# Applesauce

Applesauce belongs to all meals and all courses in the traditional Amish diet. It has most often filled the place of a salad, standing against the rich meats and mainstays, lightening their effects on stomachs.

Applesauce may be served *with* dessert, but seldom *alone* as dessert. It accompanies cake and cookies well. In fact, some Amish cooks admit to mixing applesauce and apple butter to fill their schnitz pies rather than beginning from scratch with dried apple slices.

Applesauce goes well with fried potatoes, scrapple and eggs for breakfast. It even works as a snack — ladled over hot toast!

*Fresh* applesauce is best, contend these aficionados. The fruit press stands ready in the cellar stairway of many Amish kitchens, since the apples that drop from the trees in the yard or orchard furnish enough for day-to-day use.

Each cook knows which apple makes the sauce her family most enjoys. When that apple comes into season she gears up for a major producing-canning operation. It is the moment to secure a year's-worth of applesauce for family and guests.

> 5 lbs. ripe apples
> 3 cups water
> 1-1½ cups sugar

Cut apples in half and core. Remove any spots, then cut apples in quarters.

Put apples in deep, heavy saucepan. Add water and cook. Stir occasionally to keep cooking even throughout and to prevent apples from sticking.

When apples are thoroughly soft, pour into food press, standing in a large pan. Press apples through sieve and stir in sugar (lesser amount initially) while sauce is still warm so sugar dissolves. Taste. Add more sugar if needed.

Allow to cool and serve, or pour into canning jars while still hot and process.

# Fruit Salad

This dish is so dependent upon whatever is available, either in the garden, local orchard or canning shelves, that a recipe for it is almost needless. Nonetheless, it is a treat, reserved for special occasions because of the vast amount of chopping it requires.

Certain fruits are regarded as basics and should be present, if at all possible, in balance with each other:

**apples (use several varieties with peelings on to add color)**
**peaches, fresh or canned**
**pears, fresh or canned**
**apricots, fresh or canned**
**bananas**
**grapes, any variety, but seeded**

Other fruits may be added in lesser amounts as available:

**strawberries**
**sweet cherries, seeded**
**blueberries**
**raspberries**
**plums**

Cut each large fruit in small pieces. Fold all together gently. Use at least one or two canned fruits so the salad is juicy rather than dry.

Add the apples and bananas just before serving so they do not darken or get mushy.

# Pickled Relishes, Sweets and Sours

The Pennsylvania German palate requires a sweet and sour accompaniment to its rich meats as surely as it demands gravy with mashed potatoes. That combination is an historical practice; it is also a digestive principle.

In the early 19th century the flavoring used in combination with marbled and fatty meats was primarily acidic and tart. Unsweetened fruits, pickles in sharp vinegar dressings and sauerkraut were served side by side with salted and smoked meats.[4] A woman in her mid-80s explained the easy access the cook had to vinegar. "We made cider and whatever didn't get drunk we would put in a barrel and it would turn sour. Sometimes it wouldn't work; then we'd add a little old vinegar and that would turn it. We kept it up in the barn in a barrel with a spigot on it. It would get so strong we would use only about half of what the recipe called for."

Acculturation may explain the gradual influx of sweetened fruits and vinegars into the Pennsylvania German diet at the beginning of the 20th century. Influenced by the wealthy, urban society in Philadelphia, these peddler farmers learned about sweetening the syrups in which they preserved their fruits and vegetables. Sugar in a more refined form became increasingly available at economical prices following the Spanish-American War, when Puerto Rico and the Philippines came under United States government jurisdiction.[5]

That development, coupled with these people's abundantly productive gardens and orchards and historical taste preferences, has kept pickled relishes on the tables of many Amish households ever since. The "seven sweets and seven sours" myth is an exaggeration, however, of this practice which carries on today, yet in a much more moderate manner.

One woman in her mid-30s explains, "When we had company, or when we went away, there was always a greater variety of pickled dishes served than we had day-to-day. At home we often had pickles or cole slaw or stuffed peppers, but we didn't nearly always. For church lunch now we always eat red beets and pickles, often two kinds of sweet ones."

An elderly woman, born at the turn of the 20th century, reflected on the changes she has been a part of. "When we have company we like to have pickles or something sour. But ordinarily during the week we don't have it because we use more mayonnaise. We can get lettuce year around so we eat many more salads. Years ago we always had pickles or red beets or chow chow. Or applesauce. You just felt better."

Another old practice was to keep a cruet of vinegar on the table so that a few splashes could be added to the cooked vegetables after they had been dished onto individuals' plates. "A little is good," smiles one middle-aged woman.

Horseradish, that powerfully flavored root, also appeared regularly on the table as a foil to the richest meats or to bring some zest to certain bland dishes. Older people still relish it. A man in his early 70s recalls, "We grew our own horseradish. It made you cry twice—once when you grated it and prepared it; again when you ate it! We put it on sausage, mush and puddin's, scrapple. That's just the way it was always done!"

A hearty grandmother remarked, "We like horseradish. But it's so hard to process; grinding it makes you cry! I like it, though, on most anything—sandwiches, mush and puddin's. We ate it a little like ketchup."

One woman in her early 40s, who still grows her own horseradish (although many today buy it already processed), uses it on eggs and meat. When mixed with vinegar and spices, horseradish, with its sharp, acidic flavor, is reminiscent of those early tart fruits and vegetables savored in combination with heavy meat dishes. The tradition, although tempered, continues.

# Fourteen Day Sweet Pickles

2 gallons small cucumbers
1½ cups salt to 1 gallon cold water
2 Tbsp. powdered alum
8 cups granulated sugar
8 cups apple cider vinegar
3 cups water
1 Tbsp. celery seed
2 Tbsp. mixed pickling spices
1 Tbsp. whole allspice
2 oz. cinnamon sticks

Wash cucumbers well. Cut off the stem ends into the flesh of the cucumbers, so the brine and syrup can penetrate them thoroughly. Place in large dishpan or crock. Dissolve salt in water and pour over cucumbers, being sure that all are fully submerged. Weight the cover in order to keep cucumbers under the brine. Let set for 6 days.

On day 7 drain the cucumbers, then prick each one 3 times with a sharp fork or paring knife tip. This allows further penetration of the pickles with the brine to prevent shrivelling and wrinkling. Cover with fresh boiling water.

On day 8 drain the pickles and cover again with fresh boiling water.

On day 9 drain the pickles. Mix the alum with fresh boiling water and pour over pickles, being sure they are covered.

On day 10, drain the pickles and cover them with fresh boiling water. When the mixture reaches room temperature, drain the pickles again.

Mix together 2 cups of sugar, all the vinegar and all the spices (place in a cheesecloth bag to make removal easier). Bring to a boil, then pour over the pickles.

On day 11 drain the pickles and reserve the syrup. Stir in 2 more cups of sugar into the syrup, bring to a boil and pour over the pickles. Repeat this process on days 12 and 13, each day adding 2 more cups of sugar.

On day 14 drain all the syrup into a saucepan and bring to a boil. Meanwhile spoon the pickles into hot sterilized jars. Pour boiling syrup into each jar to cover the pickles, then seal.

# Seven Day Sweet Pickles

7 lbs. medium-sized cucumbers (about 3″ long)
boiling water
1 quart apple cider vinegar
8 cups granulated sugar
2 Tbsp. salt
2 Tbsp. mixed pickling spices

Scrub the pickles, put them in a large dishpan or crock and cover them with boiling water. Let stand for 24 hours. On day 2 drain them, then cover them again with fresh boiling water. Repeat that process on days 3 and 4.

On day 5 drain the pickles, then cut them into ¼″ slices. Combine the vinegar, sugar and seasonings and bring to a boil. Pour over the sliced pickles. On day 6 drain the syrup into a saucepan, bring to a boil and pour over the pickles once again. Repeat that process on day 7, then spoon the pickles and syrup into hot sterilized jars and seal.

*Makes about 7 pints*

# Sweet Pickles

(short process)

1 gallon medium-sized cucumbers, cut in 1″ chunks
½ cup salt
boiling water
3 cups granulated sugar
3 cups apple cider vinegar
1 cup water
½ tsp. turmeric
1 tsp. dry mustard
1 tsp. allspice
1 tsp. mustard seed
1 tsp. celery seed

Combine cucumber chunks and salt. Place in large dishpan or crock and add boiling water to cover. Let stand overnight, then drain.

Mix together sugar, vinegar and spices in a large saucepan. When it comes to a boil add the pickles and return to the boiling point.

Spoon into hot sterilized jars and seal.

*Makes 8 pints*

# Bread and Butter Pickles

1 gallon thinly sliced, medium-sized cucumbers, unpared
6 – 8 medium-sized onions, thinly sliced
2 green peppers, chopped
1/3 cup salt
4 1/2 cups granulated sugar
2 Tbsp. mustard seed
1 1/2 tsp. turmeric
1 1/2 tsp. celery seed
4 1/2 cups vinegar

Gently mix together the cucumbers, onions, green peppers and salt. Cover with crushed ice and let stand for 3 hours. Continue to add ice as it melts so cucumbers become crisp and cold.

Drain well. Meanwhile, combine sugar, spices and vinegar in a large kettle and bring to a boil. Add drained vegetables and heat to boiling point, but do not boil.

Spoon into hot sterilized jars and seal.

*Makes 8 pints*

# Chow Chow

This canning project works well in late summer as gardening begins to wind down. Chow chow does not require the youngest, tiniest vegetables, so it is a way to use the last of the season's yield.

In some families, sisters get together for chow-chow making. That relieves the tedium of chopping and cooking the numerous vegetables that go into the most subtly favored, variously textured and brightly colored chow chow.

> 4 cups lima beans
> 4 cups green string beans
> 2 cups yellow wax beans
> 4 cups cabbage, chopped
> 4 cups cauliflower florets
> 4 cups carrots, sliced
> 4 cups celery, cut in chunks
> 4 cups red and green peppers, chopped
> 4 cups small white onions
> 4 cups cucumbers, cut in chunks
> 4 cups corn kernels
> 4 cups granulated sugar
> 3 cups apple cider vinegar
> 1 cup water
> 1 Tbsp. pickling spices
> 1 Tbsp. mustard seed
> 1 Tbsp. celery seed

Cook each vegetable separately until tender but not mushy. When each is finished lift out of hot water with a slotted spoon, and rinse with cold water to stop its cooking and preserve its color. Drain, then layer into a large dishpan.

Combine the sugar, vinegar, water and spices in a 15-quart stockpot (or do half a batch at a time in an 8-quart kettle) and bring to a boil. Make sure the sugar is fully dissolved, then spoon all the vegetables (or half of them, depending upon the size of the kettle) into the syrup and boil for 5 minutes. Stir gently, only to mix the vegetables well.

Spoon into hot sterilized jars and seal.

# Corn Relish

2 quarts corn kernels
1 quart cabbage, chopped
1 cup sweet red peppers, chopped
1 cup sweet green peppers, chopped
1 cup onions, diced
2 cups granulated sugar
4 cups apple cider vinegar
1 cup water
1 tsp. celery seed
1 tsp. mustard seed
1 Tbsp. salt
1 tsp. turmeric
1 tsp. dry mustard

Cook corn on cobs submerged in boiling water for 5 minutes. Plunge into cold water to stop cooking and preserve color. Drain, then cut from cobs. Mix gently with other vegetables.

Combine sugar, vinegar, water and spices (making sure sugar is dissolved). Pour over vegetables and simmer for 20 minutes or until vegetables are tender but not mushy.

Spoon into hot sterilized jars and seal.

*Makes about 6 pints*

# Tomato Relish

18 ripe firm tomatoes
1 stalk celery
4 medium-sized onions
2 green sweet peppers
2 red sweet peppers
⅓ cup salt
2¼ cups granulated sugar
½ tsp. ground cloves
2 tsp. cinnamon
½ tsp. black pepper
2 Tbsp. mustard seed, in cheesecloth bag
1½ cups apple cider vinegar

Peel tomatoes, then chop into small pieces. Chop celery, onions and peppers finely.

Mix together the vegetables and salt. Place in refrigerator overnight. Drain thoroughly in the morning.

Combine sugar, spices and vinegar, making sure the sugar is dissolved, in a large saucepan. Bring to a boil and simmer 3 minutes. Add vegetables and return to boil. Simmer for 10 more minutes, stirring occasionally. Remove cheesecloth bag.

Spoon into hot sterilized jars and seal.

# Ketchup

4 gallons ripe tomatoes
2 onions
5 stalks celery
2 green sweet peppers
3 cups granulated sugar
2 cups apple cider vinegar
¼ tsp. ground cloves
½ tsp. allspice
½ tsp. cinnamon
3 Tbsp. salt

Cook tomatoes, onions, celery and peppers together until soft and mushy. Force through food press or strainer.

Place strained mixture in soup kettle and add remaining ingredients. Boil 10 minutes.

Pour into hot, sterilized jars and seal.

*Makes about 6 pints*

# Garden Relish

2 gallons cucumbers
12 medium-sized onions
4 green peppers
2 medium-sized carrots
¼ cup salt
6 cups granulated sugar
4 cups apple cider vinegar
12 whole cloves
1 Tbsp. mustard seed
2 Tbsp. turmeric

Grind cucumbers, onions, peppers and carrots together until fine. Stir in salt and let set overnight.

Drain well. Mix in remaining ingredients. Place cloves and mustard seed in cloth bags. Bring to boil and simmer gently for 30 minutes. Remove bag of spices.

Spoon into the hot sterilized jars and seal.

*Makes about 12 pints*

# Pepper Relish

6 red peppers
6 yellow peppers
6 green peppers
6 small onions
½ cup celery, chopped
boiling water
½ cup brown sugar
½ cup granulated sugar
2 tsp. salt
1½ cups apple cider vinegar
½ cup water

Grind peppers, onions and celery until fine. Cover with boiling water, let set for 5 minutes, then drain.

Meanwhile, mix together remaining ingredients, being sure sugars are completely dissolved. Bring to boil, add ground vegetables and simmer for 12 minutes.

Spoon into hot sterilized jars and seal.

# Pickled Peppers

3 lbs. green, red and yellow peppers
2½ cups white distilled vinegar
2½ cups water
1¼ cups granulated sugar
8 gloves garlic
2 tsp. salt

Combine vinegar, water and sugar. Heat to boiling.

Wash peppers. Cut into ½″ strips. Place pepper strips in bowl and add enough boiling water to cover them. Cover bowl and let stand exactly 5 minutes. Drain.

Pack peppers into hot, sterilized pint jars. Place 1 garlic clove and ¼ tsp. salt in each jar. Pour hot liquid over peppers and seal.

# Sandwich Spread

(to can or feed fresh to a crowd)

6 cups cucumbers
4 cups onions
3 red sweet peppers
3 green peppers
½ cup salt
2 cups apple cider vinegar
½ cup butter or margarine
3 cups granulated sugar
3 Tbsp. flour
4 eggs, beaten
1 tsp. mustard seed
1 tsp. celery seed
1 cup cream

Grind cucumbers, onions and sweet peppers until fine. Mix salt thoroughly with vegetables. Let set for 2 hours.

Mix salted vegetables and vinegar in a saucepan and bring to a boil. Drain (reserving vinegar) and press until dry.

Blend butter or margarine, sugar, flour, eggs, spices and reserved vinegar. Stir in vegetables and simmer for 5 minutes. Add cream and bring mixture to a boil.

Pack into hot sterilized jars and seal.

# Pickled Red Beets

20 medium-sized red beets
2½ cups apple cider vinegar
2½ cups beet juice
1 cup granulated sugar
2 tsp. salt
10 whole cloves
2 cinnamon sticks

Scrub beets and remove tops. Cook beets until tender. Drain and reserve beet juice. Remove skins and cut beets into chunks.

Combine vinegar, juice, sugar and spices. Bring to a boil. Remove spices.

Add beet chunks and boil again. Pour into hot sterilized jars and seal.

# Red Beet Eggs

6 hard-boiled eggs, peeled
2½ cups leftover sweet and sour red beet juice syrup

Pour cool syrup over cooked and peeled eggs. Let stand overnight in refrigerator.

To serve, slice the eggs in half, lengthwise.

# Spiced Cantaloupe

2 lbs. ripe firm cantaloupe
3 cups water
1½ cups apple cider vinegar
2¼ cups granulated sugar
½ tsp. salt
¼ tsp. oil of cinnamon
¼ tsp. oil of cloves

Peel cantaloupe, remove seeds and cut into chunks. Pack gently into sterilized pint jars.

Chow Chow (page 90)

(clockwise from front center) Sticky Buns (page 110),
Potato Buns (page 106), Whole Wheat Bread (pages 102-103),
White Bread (page 102), Pecan Stickies (pages 110-111)

Combine remaining ingredients and bring to a boil. Let cool to room temperature.

Pour syrup into jars of cantaloupe, filling to 1″ from top. Place self-sealing lid and screw ring on each jar. Place jars in home canner, bring water to boil and boil for 15 minutes.

# Spiced Watermelon Rind

5 pounds watermelon rind, cut in 2″ chunks, each with about a ¼″ strip of pink watermelon fruit
½ cup salt
2 quarts water
5 cups granulated sugar
2 cups apple cider vinegar
1½ cups water
⅛ tsp. oil of cloves
⅛ tsp. oil of cinnamon

Place watermelon chunks in large dishpan or crock. Combine salt with 2 quarts of water and pour over the watermelon. Let set overnight.

Drain, rinse with fresh water and drain again.

Place watermelon in large saucepan, add fresh water and cook until tender. Drain. Meanwhile, combine sugar, vinegar, water and spices. Bring to a boil and pour over the cooked and drained watermelon. Let set overnight.

Drain watermelon, reserving syrup. Bring to boil, pour over watermelon and let set again overnight. Repeat this process for 3 days.

On day 3, cook the watermelon and syrup together for 3 minutes. Then pour into hot sterilized jars and seal.

*Makes 6 pints*

# Breads

Breadbaking is on its way back, at least among many Amish women today. When home-delivered, "bought" bread became available, the Amish were as eager customers for it as were their non-Amish neighbors. The reason? "In the outdoor bakeovens, as well as in the ovens of ranges, you couldn't control the temperature," recalls one Amish cook. "What's more, the flour wasn't as good as it is today. And the yeast certainly wasn't!"

Immediately after its baking, the bread from bakeovens and ranges was tasty and pleasing in its texture. "But they used a lot of flour and it got dry pretty quickly. I work with a lot stickier dough than they used to," comments an Amish woman in her mid-thirties. She learned to bake bread from her grandmother-in-law because her mother bought their family's bread.

Few outdoor bakeovens remain today. Those early structures were built with their own chimneys and drafts and were often covered with a roof. Their size made possible the baking of many loaves of bread at once, an efficiency measure for a cook with many children and frequently a farmhand or two to feed. It also meant that baking needed to be done only once a week, usually on Friday, so that there was fresh bread for the weekend. The bread that remained until the next baking day, however, was no one's favorite! Perhaps some weary, dry-bread eater first discovered both the pleasures of "dunking" (see page 137) and Cold Bread Soup (page 42)!

In the late 1800s some bakeovens were built with their openings in the wash houses which were attached to the farmhouses. Others were part of the farms' shop buildings where tools were kept. Those few people who recall the presence of bakeovens remember that they were used in a limited way, or not at all. "We did our baking for church in the bakeoven," a woman born in the mid-1940s explained. (The fact that so many loaves could be baked at once, and that they were eaten within a day of their baking, made the use of the bakeoven acceptable for that function.) "After the oven had cooled down somewhat, Mother would put field corn in there on racks to dry (in preparation for cornmeal) and also snitz for pies."

Another woman, born in 1904, remembers that a bakeoven stood on her grandparents' farm, but was not used within her memory. "I know that when I was a child we would open the gate in our front yard for the baker who would give each of us a cookie! It was so much work to bake bread then. I remember the 5¢ loaf. It was no wonder people didn't make their own!"

Furthermore, during the summertime when bread didn't keep as well because of the heat, and when there were more helpers around because of the extra field work, baking needed to be done twice a week. That task, even using the more modern range, was a steamy chore. There was simply little incentive for home breadbaking.

In the early to mid-1950s, numbers of Amish women began making their own bread. An Amish historian believes that change may have been related to the development of "wrapped bought bread." The loaves he remembers his mother buying when he was a child were made with yeast, were unsliced and were baked fast to the loaves on either side of it. But along with the packaging of bread some years later came the use of "unusual ingredients" instead of yeast. That change, along with the availability of improved yeast for home baking (no more trips to the old neighbor woman who grew and kept the homemade yeast!), more evenly textured flour, and stoves with refined calibration, triggered an interest in breadbaking among many Amish cooks.

The women may have been ready to swing into baking bread, but the men were not ready to eat it. Recalls one cook, "When we started baking bread we had to train the men to eat something other than bought white bread! We had all learned that a sandwich with homemade bread at school was not something we appreciated."

Another remembers, "When we were first married I wanted to bake all our own bread. But my husband said, 'Nothin' doin!' My dad always preferred bought bread, too."

In time the Amish cooks who wanted to bake yeast breads have proven their skills. Their families' tastes have been converted.

# White Bread

The Old Order Amish meet in homes for their Sunday morning services. The hosting family, with the assistance of neighbors and extended family, prepares a lunch for all who have attended.

An Amish mother of nine grown children explains, "Now for church we use homemade bread. Years ago we bought it. But it's cheaper to make our own — and better. We help each other so that whoever has church doesn't need to make it all."

½ cup lukewarm water
1 package yeast
1 tsp. sugar
2 cups lukewarm water
1¼ tsp. salt
⅓ cup sugar
1¾ Tbsp. shortening
7 – 8 cups flour

Dissolve the yeast and sugar in the ½ cup lukewarm water. Mix the 2 cups water, salt, sugar and shortening. Then add the yeast mixture and, gradually, the flour. Knead until smooth and elastic. Place in a greased bowl, cover and set in a warm place to rise until double.

Punch down. Let rise again. Put in two large loaf pans or three medium ones. Let rise until double again. Bake at 350° for ½ hour.

*Makes 2 large or 3 medium loaves*

# Whole Wheat Bread

Reflecting the more health-conscious attitude of many Amish cooks today, this recipe uses honey in place of sugar and whole wheat flour instead of all white flour.

2 packages dry yeast
4 cups warm water
½ cup margarine or butter, softened
¼ cup molasses

½ cup honey
2 tsp. salt
6 cups whole wheat flour
4 cups white flour

Dissolve yeast in warm water.

Combine margarine, molasses, honey and salt and mix well. Add yeast mixture.

Gradually add flour. Turn dough onto floured board and knead until smooth, about 7–10 minutes.

Place in greased bowl and let rise until double. Punch down. Let dough rest a few minutes.

Shape into 4 loaves. Place in greased bread pans and let rise about 1 hour.

Bake at 375° for 35–40 minutes.

# Yeast Buns

3 packages dry yeast
1 cup lukewarm water
2 cups milk
½ cup lard or vegetable oil
½ cup sugar
7–8 cups flour
1 Tbsp. salt

Dissolve the yeast in the lukewarm water. Set aside. Scald milk and add the shortening and sugar to it. Let cool to lukewarm, then add yeast mixture to it.

Beat in 3½–4 cups flour. Let rest in warm place for ½ hour.

Beat in salt and remaining flour. Knead on lightly floured surface until the dough is no longer sticky. Let rise until double in bulk.

Punch down, then form into balls the size of a large walnut. Place in a greased baking pan and let rise again until nearly double.

Bake at 400° for 15–20 minutes or until golden brown.

*Makes 3–3½ dozen rolls*

# Corn Bread

"Mother made a shortcake—not a yeast bread—with corn-meal. We ate it hot and always with canned sour cherries for our snack meal or Saturday dinnertime."

¾ cup roasted yellow cornmeal
1 cup flour
¼ cup sugar
¾ tsp. salt
3½ tsp. baking powder
1 cup milk
1 egg, beaten
¼ cup vegetable oil or lard, melted

Stir together dry ingredients.

Mix liquid ingredients together. Make a well in the dry ingredients, then add liquid all at once. Beat thoroughly.

Pour into greased 8″ square cake pan. Bake at 400° for 25–30 minutes. Serve warm.

*Makes 1 8-inch pan*

# Potato Bread

3½ cups milk
6 Tbsp. sugar
6 Tbsp. butter
2 tsp. salt
½ cup mashed potatoes
2 packages dry yeast
½ cup lukewarm water
3 cups whole wheat flour
7 – 8 cups white flour

Scald milk. Add sugar, butter, salt and mashed potatoes. Cool to lukewarm.

Meanwhile, dissolve yeast in water. Add to cooled milk mixture.

Add whole wheat flour and 1 cup white flour. Beat 2 minutes with mixer. Stir in 6 – 7 more cups flour until dough leaves sides of bowl.

Turn onto lightly floured surface. Knead gently until dough forms a smooth ball. Place in greased bowl. Turn once to grease top of dough. Cover and let rise in a warm place away from drafts until doubled, 1½ – 2 hours. Punch down and let rise again until double.

Turn onto floured surface and divide dough into 3 equal parts. Cover and let rest 10 minutes.

Form into 3 loaves and place in greased bread pans.

Bake at 350° for 40 – 45 minutes. Remove from pans and place on rack to cool.

*Makes 3 loaves*

# Potato Buns and Doughnuts

Someone learned that adding mashed potatoes to the dough for rolls and doughnuts created an appetizing softness in the finished delicacy. Now the Amish baker makes more mashed potatoes than she believes her family can eat at the main meal — "planned" leftovers, with a pleasing destination!

1 cup sugar
1 cup mashed potatoes
½ cup lard or shortening
3 eggs, beaten
1½ tsp. salt
1½ – 2 packs yeast
1 cup warm water
5 cups flour

Mix together well the sugar, potatoes, lard, eggs and salt.

Dissolve the yeast in 1 cup warm water; then add that to the above mixture.

Stir in about 3 cups of flour. Add the remaining 2 cups flour while kneading. Knead until the dough is no longer sticky but moist.

Let rise until doubled.

*For Potato Buns:*

Roll out dough to a ¾″ – 1″ thickness. Cut into bun shapes with a jar or doughnut cutter (or clover leaf — or crescent-shaped cutter) and put on greased cookie sheets about 2 inches apart. Let them rise until puffy but not doubled (they should not be touching).

Brush with milk. Bake at 325° until lightly golden brown, about 12 minutes.

*Makes about 3 dozen*

*For Doughnuts:*

Roll out dough to a ½″ thickness. Cut out with a doughnut cutter; then place on clean towels laid over cookie sheets or boards. Let rise until almost double; then fry in fat, heated to 350°–375°, about 4 inches deep. Keep fat at that temperature throughout the frying. Turn doughnuts once while frying, when they turn golden brown.

*Makes about 3½ dozen*

### Doughnut Glaze

1 lb. 10x sugar
½ cup rich milk (or a bit more)
1 Tbsp. soft butter
1 tsp. vanilla

Heat together just until butter is melted and milk is warm. Glaze while doughnuts are hot.

# Cinnamon Flop

1 cup sugar
2 cups flour
2 tsp. baking powder
1 Tbsp. melted butter
1 cup milk
brown sugar, cinnamon and butter for top

Sift sugar, flour and baking powder together. Add butter and milk and stir until well blended.

Divide mixture between 2 9″ pie or cake pans, well greased.

Sprinkle tops with flour, then brown sugar, then cinnamon. Push chunks of butter into the dough. This makes holes and later gets gooey as it bakes. Bake at 350° for 30 minutes.

Cut into wedges and serve warm.

*Makes 2 9″ pans*

# Glazed Doughnuts

One tradition that continued among those women who mastered the earlier, less desirable flour and yeast, was doughnut-making. They mixed yeast doughs, then shaped them with a hole in the middle. An elderly Amish man remembers, "We'd have doughnuts at Christmastime or during butchering season when there was lard around. But I didn't know anything of *fastnachts* because we didn't keep Lent." In that, the Amish stand in contrast to their neighboring Pennsylvania Germans who are from a higher church tradition. Those folks, on Shrove Tuesday, bake fastnachts (a doughnut without a center hole, that is fried in lard) in a symbolic effort to rid their homes of leavening agents, and to feast before Lent.

A 40-year-old Amish woman fears that homemade doughnut-making may become a lost skill. "My mother made good doughnuts. She'd be asked to make the kind with holes in the middle for weddings. But now the young folks buy filled ones."

1 cake yeast
1 cup warm water
1 cup scalded milk
½ cup sugar
1 tsp. salt
7 cups flour, sifted
½ cup melted lard or shortening
2 eggs
1 tsp. vanilla

Dissolve yeast in warm water. Mix milk, sugar and salt together. Cool to lukewarm. Add yeast mixture to milk.

Add 4 cups flour, one cup at a time, beating well after each addition.

Stir in lard, eggs and vanilla. Add 3 more cups flour. Knead until smooth.

Let rise until doubled, about 2½ hours. Punch down, then roll to ½-inch thickness on floured surface.

Cut out doughnuts with doughnut cutter. Lay on clean towels over cookie sheets and let rise again until nearly double. Deep-fry in fat at 350°–375°. Glaze while warm. (See Glaze recipe on p. 107.)

*Makes about 5 dozen*

# Cream Filled Doughnuts

¾ cup lard or shortening
¾ cup sugar
1 cup hot water
1 cup warm water
2 packages dry yeast
2 eggs, beaten
1 tsp. salt
6 or more cups flour

In large bowl combine shortening, sugar and hot water. Add yeast to warm water and set aside to dissolve.

When shortening mixture has cooled, add eggs, salt, yeast mixture and flour.

Turn dough onto floured surface and knead until smooth and elastic. Cover and set in a warm place. Let rise until double. Roll dough about ½" thick and cut with drinking glass or doughnut cutter without the hole. Let rise again until double.

Fry doughnuts in deep fat until browned, turning once. Cool and fill.

To fill, cut a small hole with a sharp knife. Force filling into doughnut with a cookie press or cake decorator.

*Filling*

4 cups 10x sugar
1½ cups shortening
2 egg whites
2 Tbsp. flour
2 tsp. vanilla
4 Tbsp. milk

Combine all ingredients and beat until smooth.

*Makes 2½ dozen*

# Sticky Buns

These breakfast favorites are also commonly known as Sweet Rolls, Cinnamon Rolls or Pecan Stickies. The basic sweet roll dough adapts easily to varied glazes and fillings.

These buns have made satisfying snacks before the late afternoon milking. They also pack well into school lunch boxes.

> 1 package dry yeast
> 1/4 cup warm water
> 1/4 cup shortening
> 1/4 cup sugar
> 1 cup milk, scalded, or 1 cup warm water
> 1 tsp. salt
> 1 egg, beaten
> 3 1/4 – 4 cups flour

Dissolve yeast in warm water.

In large bowl, cream shortening and sugar. Pour hot milk or water over mixture. Cool to lukewarm. Add 1 cup flour and beat well. Beat in yeast mixture and egg.

Gradually add remaining flour to form a soft dough, beating well.

Brush top of dough with softened margarine or butter. Cover and let rise in warm place until double (1 1/2 – 2 hours).

Punch down and knead. Form rolls. Let rise again until doubled. Bake according to instructions below.

*For Cinnamon Rolls:*

Divide dough in half. Roll each half into a rectangle, approximately 12″ × 8.″ Spread with butter and sprinkle with a mixture of 1/2 cup brown sugar and 1 tsp. cinnamon. Roll as a jelly roll. Cut into 1 – 1 1/2″ slices. Place rolls in greased pans about 3/4″ apart. Let rise and bake at 350° for 30 minutes. Cool and spread with doughnut glaze (see page 107).

*For Raisin Cinnamon Rolls:*

Make rolls as above, but sprinkle with raisins before rolling up. Bake as above.

### For Pecan Stickies:

Place ½ cup pecans in bottom of each of two greased 9½ × 5 × 3″ pans. Make syrup by heating slowly: ½ cup brown sugar, ¼ cup butter and 1 Tbsp. light corn syrup. Pour half of syrup over each pan of pecans. Prepare Cinnamon Rolls, using only ¼ cup brown sugar, and place rolls on top of pecans and syrup.

Let rise till double and bake at 375° for about 25 minutes. Remove from oven and turn pan upside down onto a flat plate.

Syrup will run down through the rolls and pecans will be on top.

*Makes 2 dozen*

# Waffles

Waffles are a rare treat; after all, how can one cook keep many hungry mouths happy with only one waffle iron? Some women tried, under less than ideal conditions!

"I remember Mother making waffles on the range," one graying grandmother smiled. "She would take the lid off and fit a round waffle iron down into the 'burner' opening above the flame on the range. It was a messy business, and hard to have the fire just right, so she didn't do it very often. And those were heavy waffles!"

Here is a lighter version that holds up under chicken gravy for a main meal or thickened fruit sauce for breakfast or a snack.

**4 eggs**
**2½ cups milk**
**¾ cup melted shortening**
**3½ cups flour**
**6 tsp. baking powder**
**1 tsp. salt**

Combine all ingredients and beat for 1 minute.
Bake waffles in hot waffle iron.

*Makes 10 – 12 waffles*

# Bread Filling

Bread crusts or stale bread is not a problem to the resourceful Amish cook. Said one, "I just turn the crust to the inside when I'm making sandwiches and it doesn't make a difference to anyone!" But when bread passes its prime for eating as fresh slices, it is often dried to a crisp, then rolled into bread crumbs, or cubed and fashioned into Bread Filling.

A watchful cook can make this successfully on top of the stove. In fact, as one experienced Amish woman explained, "You don't even need gravy with it if you have it real moist." The dish is less likely to scorch, however, if it is baked in the oven.

4 eggs
2 cups milk
2 quarts soft bread cubes
4 Tbsp. melted butter
1 tsp. onion, minced
1 tsp. salt
1 Tbsp. parsley, chopped (optional)
1 tsp. sage or poultry seasoning (optional)

Beat eggs. Add milk. Pour over bread cubes.

Combine butter and seasonings. Add to bread cubes and mix well.

Filling can be baked in a casserole dish at 350° for 45 minutes or may be used as stuffing for fowl.

If baking in a casserole, cover tightly for the first 30 minutes, then remove cover to allow browning during the last 15 minutes of baking.

*Makes 6 servings*

# Mashed Potato Filling

Almost a vegetable dish, this soft filling was likely invented by a cook who wanted to use up leftover mashed potatoes and stale bread. The final consistency of this traditional food is pudding-like.

½ cup butter
½ cup celery, chopped
2 Tbsp. onion, chopped
4 cups soft bread cubes
½ cup boiling water
3 eggs, beaten
2 cups milk
1½ tsp. salt
2 cups mashed potatoes

Melt butter. Add celery and onion. Cook until tender. Pour over bread cubes and mix well.

Add boiling water to bread and mix well. Add remaining ingredients, mixing well after each addition. The finished product should be very moist.

Turn into 2 well greased casserole dishes. Bake at 350° for 45 minutes.

*Makes 10 servings*

# Pies

The German settlers brought their love of pastries to Pennsylvania. What they learned from their English neighbors in the New World was how to fashion that fondness into pies. And pies have been on Amish menus ever since.

Considered nearly as essential as bread, pies were part of the weekly baking. A woman born in the 1920s remembers that her grandmother regularly baked twenty pies every Friday. "There were six children at home, plus a hired man. She always made shoofly and the rest were two-crust fruit pies. That's what they filled up on!"

Another woman of similar age explains, "I was the fifth oldest of sixteen children, the second girl. My older sister got married when I was fourteen so I had to take over the cooking. It took three pies for each meal. So when I baked, I'd make eight shoofly pies, eight pumpkin and eight crumb pies."

In the Amish food tradition, pies have always defied confinement to one particular course or one meal or time of day. An 80-year-old grandmother says, "We ate our pies hot as a main meal." She also acknowledges that change has come. "We do that now with apple dumplings, but that's about all. We ate more starch then than we do now."

Pie is still commonly eaten as a breakfast food. Shoofly is often served, and with it, canned or fresh fruit and milk.

Pies are kept on tap as an accompaniment to soup, for dessert, for a pre-milking pick-up, for a bedtime snack. Pie is a tradition that has proven its adaptability through the years, even into this more health-conscious age. Most fruit pies can be made without a top crust, for example. Vegetable oil can be substituted for lard in the crust and the sugar content reduced in the filling. Too much tampering, however, can frustrate both the memory and experience of eating good pie! Here, then, are the old recipes.

# Pie Crust

The batter-stained, hand-written old cookbooks, stashed in the kitchen drawers of most Amish cooks, seldom contained instructions about how to make pie dough. If anything was there it was a list of ingredients rather than a procedure. Those directions simply weren't needed. Mothers and grandmothers taught their daughters by *showing* them, and urging them to "feel" when the dough was right. But as one mother lamented, "A number of our girls work away from home now. When I learned to cook I was between 11 and 15. I tell our one daughter, who is a school-teacher, that she must make at least one main meal a week so that she gets practice, and so she learns from me what she can before she's responsible for cooking for her own family."

4 cups flour
¾ tsp. salt
1 cup lard or vegetable shortening
1 egg, beaten
5 Tbsp. cold water
1 Tbsp. vinegar

Mix flour and salt. Cut in shortening until mixture resembles small peas.

Combine remaining ingredients and stir into shortening and flour. Let stand a few minutes.

Roll out dough on floured board.

*Makes 6 9" pie shells or 3 9" double-crust pies*

# Apple Pie

"We had our own apples so we ate a lot of apple pie." It is a common theme when one probes the subject of the kinds of pies most often baked in Amish kitchens. Another woman in her mid-thirties explains, "We ate a lot of apple pies; Mom made them with a top crust. For a full meal we would eat apple pie with potatoes alongside that were covered with brown butter. We'd eat it on a flat plate with a little bit of milk on the apple pie."

> 6 cups apples, peeled and sliced
> ½–¾ cup sugar (depending upon the flavor of the apples)
> 2 Tbsp. flour
> ¾ tsp. cinnamon
> 2 Tbsp. lemon juice
> 1 9" unbaked pie shell and top crust

Toss apple slices gently with sugar, flour, cinnamon and lemon juice. Spoon into unbaked pie shell. Top with crust, folding its edge under the top of the bottom crust. Crimp to seal. Bake at 425° for 40–50 minutes, or until crust is golden brown.

*Makes 1 9" pie*

# Sour Cherry Pie

Sweetened sour cherries have a pungent tartness that makes them a favorite for pies. Cherry trees grow both wild and domestically in eastern Pennsylvania, so their natural presence has made their fruit an easily available dessert or main dish for a snack meal. Since cherries retain their delectable qualities even when canned, cherry pies are prepared year-round.

> 3 cups sour cherries, drained
> ½ cup cherry juice
> 1 cup sugar
> 2 Tbsp. tapioca
> ⅛ tsp. salt
> 1 Tbsp. butter or margarine
> 1 9" unbaked pie shell plus top crust or lattice strips

Mix together cherries, juice, sugar, tapioca and salt. Let stand for 15 minutes to allow thickening to begin.

Pour fruit mixture into pie shell. Dot with butter. Top with crust or lattice strips of pastry.

Bake at 425° for 15 minutes, then reduce temperature to 350° and bake an additional 35–40 minutes.

*Makes 1 9" pie*

*Variation:*

Top with Crumbs (page 128) instead of top crust.

# Rhubarb Pie

Sticking around an out-building on most Amish farms is a stand of rhubarb that puts in an appearance every spring.

Its sweetened tartness makes it a favorite in the Amish diet. Rhubarb is one more example of these people's pleasure in a zesty flavor that offsets another rich food, or whose own "bite" is only partly masked by the addition of sugar.

Rhubarb must be beloved in part because it is one of the first greens to flourish after a long winter without fresh food.

3 cups diced rhubarb
1¼ cups sugar
¼ tsp. salt
2 Tbsp. water
3 Tbsp. flour
1 Tbsp. lemon juice
2 eggs
1 9" unbaked pie shell

Place rhubarb in unbaked pie shell.

Combine remaining ingredients and stir to form a smooth paste. Pour over rhubarb.

Cover with crumbs made by mixing 3 Tbsp. flour, 3 Tbsp. sugar and 2 Tbsp. butter.

Bake at 425° for 10 minutes; then at 325° for 30 more minutes.

*Makes 1 9" pie*

# Schnitz Pie

Since apple trees, which grow abundantly in eastern Pennsylvania, produced more apples than could be eaten fresh in most households, the German settlers dried much of their fruit. It was a home operation. The apples were peeled and cut into slices ("schnitz" means to cut into pieces), then laid on a roof or on racks above a heat source to dry.

Most apples dried in 24–48 hours, depending upon the thickness of the slices, the temperature of the heat source and the temperature and humidity of the weather. Once dried, the sweet slices were stored in a dry container for use at any time of the year.

Today, schnitz pie is usually served at the lunch which follows the Sunday morning church service. It is traditionally part of the main course at the snack meal of the day when either potato soup or bean soup is on the menu (see page 36).

Schnitz is now prepared commercially in Pennsylvania, so it is available to those without their own source of fresh apples.

**3 cups dried apples**
**2¼ cups warm water**
**1 tsp. lemon extract**
**⅔ cup brown sugar**
**1 9″ unbaked pie shell plus top crust**

Soak apples in the warm water, then cook over low heat until soft. Mash apples and add lemon and sugar.

Pour into unbaked pie shell. Cover with top crust. Seal edges.

Bake at 425° for 15 minutes; then at 350° for 30 minutes. Serve warm.

*Makes 1 9″ pie*

# Half-Moon Pies

A variation on schnitz pie developed in the Big Valley area of Pennsylvania, where an Amish settlement began in 1790. The Amish, who live west and south of Lewistown in the central part of the state, fashioned a schnitz pie that travels well—in the hand or in lunch boxes! Its name is descriptive of how the finished delicacy looks.

    2 quarts dried apples
    3 cups water
    1½ cups granulated sugar
    1½ cups brown sugar
    ¾ tsp. cinnamon
    1½ tsp. allspice
    ¾ tsp. salt
    pie dough (page 117) for 4 9″ shells

Boil the dried apples in the water until the water is fully absorbed.

While they are cooking, prepare the pie dough (page 117). Then drain the apples. Blend in sugar and spices.

To form the individual pies, take a piece of dough about the size of an egg and shape it into a ball. Roll out into a circle until the dough is thin, yet able to hold the filling. Fold dough in half to form a crease through the center. Mark the top of one half with a pie crimper to shape the rounded edge.

Put ½ cup of the schnitz filling on the other half. Wet the outer edges of the dough. Fold the marked half over the half with the filling. Press edges together, cutting off ragged edges with the pie crimper.

Brush the tops with beaten egg, lift onto cookie sheets and bake at 425° until golden brown.

*Makes 2 – 2½ dozen individual pies*

# Lemon Meringue Pie

juice and grated rind of one lemon
3 Tbsp. cornstarch
1 cup sugar
3 egg yolks
1¼ cups boiling water
1 9″ baked pie shell

Add cornstarch and sugar to lemon juice and rind. Stir until smooth. Blend in egg yolks and then the boiling water.

Cook mixture in double boiler, stirring constantly until thickened.

Cool, then pour into baked pie shell. Top with meringue. Bake at 350° until lightly golden (watch carefully!).

*Meringue*

3 egg whites
4 Tbsp. sugar

Beat whites stiffly. Fold in sugar, one tablespoon at a time. Pile onto lemon pie.

*Makes 1 9″ pie*

# Lemon Sponge Pie

Lemon pies were a treat. Citrus fruit does not grow in eastern Pennsylvania. But the area's proximity to the canals, that webbed their way as far west as Ohio and provided waterways to the Atlantic coastal cities, made it possible to get lemons and oranges. Some farmers sold their hay in Philadelphia and could bring home the treats available there.

In many homes, lemon pies were made primarily when company was coming.

    1 cup sugar
    2 Tbsp. butter
    3 eggs, separated
    3 Tbsp. flour
    ½ tsp. salt
    juice and grated rind of 1 lemon
    1½ cups hot water or milk
    1 9″ unbaked pie shell

Cream sugar and butter. Add egg yolks and beat well. Add flour, salt, lemon juice and rind. Add water or milk. Fold in stiffly beaten egg whites.

Pour into unbaked pie shell. Bake at 325° for 45–50 minutes.

*Makes 1 9″ pie*

# Shoofly Pie

This cakey pie, with a name that has produced a myriad of reasons for its existence, may have its roots in the early bake-ovens of Pennsylvania. Dense cakes with heavy dough were put into the bakeovens following the weekly bread-baking, which required the hottest fires. This hybrid cake within a pie shell weathered the bakeoven well. It was with the advent of the kitchen range and its more easily controlled temperatures that lighter pies with custards, creams and more delicate fruit became common.

*Crumbs*

1 cup flour
⅔ cup light brown sugar
1 Tbsp. shortening

Mix flour and sugar. Cut in shortening. Take out ½ cup crumbs and set aside.

*Bottom Part*

1 egg, slightly beaten
1 cup molasses
1 cup boiling water
1 tsp. baking soda
1 9″ unbaked pie shell

To larger portion of crumb mixture add egg and molasses. Blend in ¾ cup boiling water. Dissolve soda in remaining ¼ cup water and add last.

Pour into unbaked pie shell. Sprinkle reserved crumbs on top. Bake at 425° for 15 minutes. Reduce heat to 350° and bake 40–45 minutes longer.

*Makes 1 9″ pie*

# Montgomery Pie

Pies with cakey tops and a variety of syrupy flavored bottoms are remembered especially by the older members of the Amish community. This cake in a pie shell is related to the more common shoofly pie, although its lemon-flavored bottom is reminiscent of lemon sponge pie.

*Bottom*

juice and grated rind of one lemon
1 cup molasses
2 cups water
1 cup sugar
3 Tbsp. flour
1 egg
3 unbaked 9″ pie shells

Blend first six ingredients until smooth. Pour into 3 pie shells.

*Top*

½ cup butter or margarine
2 cups sugar
2 eggs
1 cup milk
2½ cups flour
2½ tsp. baking powder

Cream butter and sugar. Add eggs and beat thoroughly. Combine flour and baking powder. Add milk alternately with dry ingredients.

Divide batter and pour over the syrup in the pie shells.

Bake at 450° for 15 minutes; reduce heat to 350° and continue baking another 45 minutes.

*Makes 3 9″ pies*

# Vanilla Pie

Vanilla pie is a close cousin to shoofly pie, distinct from it mostly by the presence of vanilla in the syrupy bottom part.

¼ cup granulated sugar
¼ cup brown sugar
½ cup molasses or light corn syrup
1 cup water
1 egg, well beaten
1 Tbsp. flour
1 tsp. vanilla
1 9″ unbaked pie shell

Combine all the above ingredients, *except* the vanilla, in a saucepan. Bring to a boil and continue boiling until thickened. Allow to cool and stir in vanilla. Pour into unbaked shell.

*Crumbs*

1 cup flour
½ tsp. baking powder
½ tsp. baking soda
½ cup brown sugar
¼ cup lard, butter, margarine or vegetable shortening

Melt shortening. Stir in dry ingredients. Crumble over syrup. Bake at 375° for 50–60 minutes.

*Makes 1 9″ pie*

# Pumpkin Pie

Gooseneck pumpkins grow in southeastern Pennsylvania. With some experimentation, and likely through association with their English neighbors, the German settlers discovered the pleasure of pumpkin, in combination with molasses, eggs, spices and cream. It became a regularly prepared pie in Amish homes, with little or no connection to Thanksgiving or Christmas.

1½ cups mashed pumpkin or butternut squash

1 egg
½ cup milk, heated
½ cup cream, heated
1 Tbsp. flour
1 Tbsp. molasses or King Syrup
¾ cup sugar
1 tsp. cinnamon
dash of nutmeg
1 Tbsp. brown butter
pinch of salt
1 9″ unbaked pie shell

Combine all ingredients. Pour into unbaked pie shell. Sprinkle additional cinnamon and nutmeg over top of pie.
    Bake at 450° for 15 minutes; then at 350° for 45 minutes.

*Makes 1 9″ pie*

# Custard Pie

Most Amish families' egg supplies have come from their own flocks of chickens. When there were plenty of eggs, the cook had a repertoire of dishes to make so that no eggs went to waste (fried or scrambled for breakfast or lunch, in sandwiches or on top of stewed crackers, mixed into noodles or angel food cake, and more). Custard pies were a welcome variation to the usual weekly fare.

⅓ cup sugar
2 tsp. flour
½ tsp. salt
3 eggs
3 cups milk
¼ tsp. nutmeg
1 9″ unbaked pie shell

Combine sugar, flour, salt and eggs and mix until smooth.
    Heat milk to boiling point. Add 1 cup hot milk to egg mixture. Pour that into the remaining hot milk.
    Pour into unbaked pie shell. Sprinkle nutmeg over top. Bake at 350° for 40–45 minutes.

*Makes 1 9″ pie*

# Peach Pie

From mid-July through the end of August, peaches are in full supply in eastern Pennsylvania. Family orchards produce some; fruit farms raise them in abundance.

The Amish woman cans dozens of jars of peaches, but saves many for eating fresh — simply cut in slices or over shortcake or in pies.

> **4 cups peaches, peeled and sliced**
> **½ cup sugar**
> **¼ tsp. salt**
> **2½ Tbsp. tapioca**
> **1 9″ unbaked pie shell**

Mix together gently peaches, sugar, salt and tapioca. Let blend for 5 minutes before spooning into pie shell. Top with crumbs.

Bake at 425° for 45–50 minutes.

*Makes 1 9″ pie*

*Crumbs*

> **2½ Tbsp. butter or margarine, melted**
> **¼ cup flour**
> **½ tsp. cinnamon**
> **⅓ cup brown sugar**

Mix together until crumbly and sift over pie.

# Pear Pie

Many farmsteads had a wild seckel pear tree growing somewhere on the acreage. It was the domesticated pear trees in the family orchard or on local fruit farms, however, that provided the fruit for the seasonal pear pies. Canned pears could also be used to bring occasional variety to the family's pie diet.

> **¼ cup flour**

(left to right) Apple Pie (page 118) and Rhubarb Pie (page 119)

Home-canned fruits, vegetables, and juices

¾ cup sugar
1 cup cream
1 Tbsp. lemon juice
5 fresh pears, peeled and diced, or canned pears in light
  syrup
¼ tsp. cinnamon
1 Tbsp. sugar
1 9″ unbaked pie shell

Sift together flour and sugar. Stir in cream and lemon juice.
Mix until smooth. Add pears. Pour into an unbaked pie shell.
Sprinkle top with sugar and cinnamon.
  Bake at 400° for 45–50 minutes. Cool until set.

*Makes 1 9″ pie*

# Ground-Cherry Pie

Ground-cherries grow wild in the Pennsylvania countryside.
Stewards of the earth's bounty, the Amish picked them for food,
discovering them to be tasty filling for pies.

3½ cups ground-cherries
1½ cups water
⅓ cup cornstarch
1¼ cups sugar
¼ tsp. salt
1 cup water
2 Tbsp. lemon juice
2 tsp. unflavored gelatin
⅓ cup water
1 9″ unbaked pie shell and top crust

Cook cherries in 1½ cups water until mixture comes to a boil.
Meanwhile, mix together cornstarch, sugar, salt and one cup
water until smooth. Stir into boiling cherries until fruit thickens.
  Remove from heat and stir in lemon juice.
  Soak gelatin in ⅓ cup water. Add to fruit mixture, stirring well.
  Spoon into unbaked pie shell and add top crust. Bake at 400°
for 15 minutes; reduce heat to 375° and bake 30 minutes longer.

*Makes 1 9″ pie*

# Grape Pie

Concord grape arbors shade many Amish porches. Their summer fruit yields gallons of juice, batches of jam and an occasional pie. The skins and seeds are obstacles to overcome, but the tangy flavor makes the effort worthwhile.

**3 cups Concord grapes**
**½ – ¾ cup sugar**
**3 Tbsp. flour**
**1 Tbsp. lemon juice**
**1 Tbsp. butter**
**1 9″ unbaked pie shell and top crust**

Stem grapes, wash, drain and squeeze from skins. Set skins aside. Simmer remaining pulp for 5 minutes.

Remove from heat and immediately put through food press (this will separate the seeds from the usable pulp).

Stir pulp and skins together. Blend in sugar and flour. Add lemon juice and butter.

Spoon into pie shell. Cover with top crust.

Bake at 425° for 10 minutes; reduce temperature to 350° and bake an additional 30 minutes.

*Makes 1 9″ pie*

*Variation:*

**1 cup flour**
**½ cup sugar**
**¼ cup melted butter**

Mix together until crumbly. Sprinkle over pie in place of the top crust.

# Raisin Pie

Raisin pie was not on the weekly menu. "We had to buy the raisins. It just wasn't as common as cherry because we grew our own cherries."

In contrast to some groups of Germanic heritage, the Lancaster Amish of this century do not — and have no memory of — serving raisin pie at their funerals. "We often have stewed prunes, but raisin pies are not a funeral tradition," said a minister's wife, whose explanation was corroborated by several others of varying ages.

The most traditional pie is one in which the raisins are stewed in water and that juice is thickened, rather than a cream pie to which milk is added.

> 2 cups raisins
> 2 cups cold water
> 1½ cups sugar
> 4 Tbsp. flour
> 2 eggs, separated
> ¼ tsp. salt
> 4 Tbsp. melted butter
> 1 Tbsp. vinegar or lemon juice
> 1 9″ baked pie shell

In saucepan combine raisins, 1½ cups water and 1 cup sugar and bring to a boil. Combine the remaining ½ cup water and ½ cup sugar, plus flour, egg yolks and salt; add to raisin mixture. Cook until thickened, stirring constantly. Remove from heat and add butter and vinegar or lemon juice.

Pour mixture into baked pie shell. Cover with whipped cream or meringue.

### *Meringue*

Beat egg whites till stiff peaks form. Gradually add 2 Tbsp. sugar while beating. Pile on top of pie and bake at 350° till golden brown, about 10 minutes.

*Makes 1 9″ pie*

# Huckleberry Pie

"Huckleberry picking was an outing," recalls an Amish grand-father. "We'd get up early, pack our lunches and go down to the Welsh Mountain. There had been a forest fire years before and huckleberry bushes grew up where the trees once stood.

"We would pick while the day was still cool. When it got hot we ate our lunches, picked some more, then took the berries home to can them. Often several of us families would go together."

Huckleberries are a kind of wild blueberry. Blueberries may be used in this recipe; the sugar may be adjusted depending upon the tartness of the berries.

> 2¾ cups huckleberries
> ½ cup berry juice or 3 Tbsp. lemon juice with water
>   added to make ½ cup liquid
> ½ cup sugar
> 2 Tbsp. flour
> 1 9″ unbaked pie shell and top crust

Stem and wash huckleberries. Spoon into pie shell.

Mix juice, sugar and flour together and pour over berries. Cover with top crust, folding under top edge of bottom crust.

Bake at 425° for 10 minutes. Reduce temperature to 350° and bake 30 minutes more.

*Makes 1 9″ pie*

# Mincemeat Pie

Mincemeat pie likely had its beginnings during medieval times when spiced meat dishes were the order of the day and served as the main meal rather than dessert.

It is probable that the Pennsylvania Germans learned this recipe from their English neighbors. Mincemeat pie fits well the needs of German farmers — it is a hearty meal; the meat was a by-product from home-butchering; the additional fruits could be varied according to the dried or canned supply that was in the attic or cellar.

One grandmother remembers, "We'd eat it at butchering time. But Mom canned the mincemeat so we could have it anytime. Now I think I can't make it because we don't butcher. You see, Mom would cook the beef bones and then pick off the last bits of meat. Using the bones gave the meat and broth a full flavor you don't get otherwise, and it used up every corner of the meat!"

**Beef bone yielding 2 cups cooked meat, cut in small pieces**
**1½ cups raisins**
**3 cups apples, peeled and chopped fine**
**½ cup brown sugar**
**⅓ cup fresh orange sections, cut up in small pieces**
**¼ cup fresh lemon sections, cut up in small pieces**
**¼ tsp. salt**
**1 tsp. cinnamon**
**½ tsp. cloves**
**⅓ cup cider**
**1 9″ unbaked pie shell and top crust**

Simmer beef bone until meat is tender. Cut in fine pieces. Combine beef with remaining ingredients and simmer for 10–15 minutes (add beef broth if needed to keep mixture from getting dry).

Pour into unbaked pie shell. Cover with top crust; seal edges thoroughly.

Bake at 425° for 15 minutes, then reduce temperature to 375° and bake another 35 minutes.

*Makes 1 9″ pie*

# Green Tomato Pie

Amish cooks can only speculate about the origin of green tomato pie: "In the fall people wanted to use up their excess tomatoes so they made this pie." Suggests another, "Maybe it was to help out in an emergency—'What shall we make for supper?!'" "Maybe green tomato pie developed to supplement the apple supply, which at that season of the year was nearly depleted." Another remembers, "Mother used to make it because she really liked it and so did my father. I think she made it as a special treat for him. I didn't care for it that much, but we didn't have to eat dessert! It did provide a little variety in the pies we ate."

It has been noted that the seasonings that accompany the green tomatoes are much the same as those that flavor mincemeat pie, another fall dish.

> 4 cups green tomatoes, sliced thin (leave parings on)
> 1 cup granulated sugar
> ½ cup brown sugar
> 3 Tbsp. lemon juice
> 1 tsp. cinnamon
> ½ tsp. cloves
> 1 Tbsp. butter or margarine
> 2 Tbsp. flour
> 1 9″ unbaked pie shell and top crust

Sprinkle flour over bottom of pie shell. Layer slices of tomatoes into pie plate.

Mix sugars, lemon juice and spices together. Pour over tomatoes. Dot with butter.

Cover with top crust. Bake at 425° for 15 minutes, then reduce temperature to 375° and bake an additional 30 minutes.

*Makes 1 9″ pie*

# Walnut Pie

Black walnut trees used to grow wild along the fencerows bordering many Amish farms. The wood from these trees is now in such high demand that comparatively few of them remain. Despite the fact that the nuts were difficult to shell and stained the hands of the sheller with a black acidic liquid, the nuts were freely harvested and mixed into cakes and pies.

Their flavor is strong and penetrating, so only a relative few are needed to enliven the taste of the dessert of which they are a part. This is a rich dish for special times.

   1 cup warm water
   ¾ cup molasses
   2 eggs, well beaten
   1 cup sweet milk
   4 Tbsp. flour
   ½ cup walnuts, chopped
   2 9″ baked pie crusts

Bring water and molasses to a boil. Meanwhile, stir together beaten eggs, milk and flour until smooth. Mix into water and molasses and let boil until thick.

Remove from heat and add nuts. When cool, pour into baked crusts.

*Makes 2 9″ pies*

# Pecan Pie

Pecans were a rare treat, but not unknown to the Amish because of eastern Pennsylvania's access to goods that passed through Philadelphia and Baltimore. Pecan pie is another demonstration of the preference for a salty-sweet combination of flavors found throughout the Amish diet (sweet and sour bacon salad dressing, ham and green beans with sweet and sour cole slaw, and syrup over mush and scrapple are other examples).

2 Tbsp. butter or margarine
¼ cup sugar
2 eggs
¾ cup molasses
1 Tbsp. flour
1 tsp. vanilla
pinch salt
¾ cup water
½ cup pecans
1 8″ unbaked pie shell

Cream butter, sugar and eggs. Add molasses, flour, vanilla and salt. Stir in water and pecans.

Pour into unbaked pie shell. Bake at 450° for 10 minutes, then reduce temperature to 350° for an additional 25–30 minutes.

*Makes 1 8″ pie*

# Cakes and Cookies

Cakes and cookies, while never as passionately sought after as pies, were still a fixture in the Amish pantry. They likely entered the diet later than pies since they were more dependent upon refined flour and finely tuned temperatures than were available in the early bakeovens.[6]

Perhaps it was because of those "dry" beginnings that cakes and cookies are commonly—and openly—"dunked" when served. The practice is neither regarded as poor manners nor as an insult to the cook. "Dunking is the way to eat cookies and cakes," explains an elderly woman, smiling. Individual preferences vary, of course. "We dunk cookies in milk or hot tea," offers a mother of five children, all under the age of nine. "At harvest-time," remembers an older man, "we'd get a pretty good snack at dark and then I'd dunk that in root beer." "I just prefer to take a bite and then a sip. I don't like all those crumbs floating in my coffee and water," says a middle-aged woman.

Basic to many cake batters are eggs and sweet or sour milk—ingredients in good supply on a farm. Although the Amish settlers cannot claim credit for developing these recipes, the cakes and cookies which became their favorites have been particularly well suited to their lives. Most are substantial; most require few steps in their procedures and so can be whipped up in large quantities, either for sizable families or for sale at market stands.

These cakes and cookies make hearty breakfasts, they top off any meal, they travel well in school lunches, they brighten a mid-afternoon snack in the fields.

# Chocolate Cake

"The cake we ate most at home was chocolate," reports an Amish woman with slightly graying hair. "It was usually baked in a long pan, and dusted with 10X sugar rather than iced." Her memory is echoed by many others, no matter their ages.

   1 cup brown sugar
   1 cup granulated sugar
   1 cup lard (or vegetable shortening)
   2 eggs, unbeaten
   1 cup buttermilk
   2¾ cups flour
   ½ cup cocoa powder
   ½ cup boiling water
   1 tsp. baking soda

Cream sugars and lard (or shortening). Mix in eggs, buttermilk, flour and cocoa until well blended.

Dissolve baking soda in boiling water, then stir into batter.

Pour into greased and floured round layer cake pans or into a long pan, 9″ × 13″. Bake at 350° for 25–35 minutes. Test for doneness before removing from oven.

*Makes 1 long or 1 layer cake*

# Hot Milk Sponge Cake

A woman born at the turn of the century recalls, "We baked a lot of sponge cakes." The favored cake came from Germany and continued as a specialty here. Eggs were usually plentiful and could be put to good use in this batter. The cake was also adaptable — the cook could add her choice of flavoring before baking, or she could leave it out and serve the cake with fresh strawberries (or whatever fruit was easily at hand).

Note that this cake requires no shortening.

   4 eggs
   2 cups granulated sugar
   2 tsp. flavoring (optional)

2 Tbsp. butter or margarine, melted
1 cup hot milk
2 cups flour
½ tsp. salt
2 tsp. baking powder

Beat eggs and sugar together until light. Mix together flavoring, butter or margarine and hot milk. Stir into eggs and sugar and blend thoroughly.

Sift together dry ingredients. Fold lightly into batter until smooth.

Bake in either a greased and floured 9″ × 13″ cake pan at 350° for 25–30 minutes, or in a tube pan (do *not* grease or flour) at 350° for 45 minutes.

*Makes 1 large cake*

# Ice Water White Cake

½ cup butter or margarine
2 cups granulated sugar
3½ cups cake flour
½ tsp. salt
3 tsp. baking powder
1½ cups ice water
¼ tsp. almond flavoring (optional)
4 egg whites, stiffly beaten

Cream shortening. Gradually add sugar, beating until fluffy.

Sift dry ingredients together. Add alternately with ice water and flavoring, if desired, to creamed shortening.

Fold in stiffly beaten egg whites.

Bake in 2 greased cake layer pans at 350° for 30 minutes.

*Makes 1 layer cake*

# Angel Food Cake

Angel food cakes are not an extravagance on a farm where eggs are plentiful. In fact, the cake was often baked on the same day as noodles were made. Noodles required the yolks; angel food cakes the egg whites.

An experienced cook, who learned to bake the delicacy as a 14-year-old, says that the cake turns out best if the eggs are beaten by hand rather than with an electric mixer. "If you beat the eggs too fast, the foam goes down. I always used a wire whisk at home."

This light, mildly flavored cake is enhanced when crushed strawberries are served over it.

    1½ cups cake flour
    2¼ cups granulated sugar
    2½ cups egg whites (18 eggs)
    3 Tbsp. water
    ¼ tsp. salt
    1½ tsp. cream of tartar
    1½ tsp. vanilla

Sift the flour. Add ¾ cup sugar and sift with flour three times. Set aside.

Beat the egg whites with a rotary beater (not an electric mixer) until foamy. Add salt and cream of tartar. Continue beating until the whites hold peaks. Slowly add the rest of the sugar to the beaten egg whites, folding it in gently. Add the vanilla.

Sift the flour and sugar mixture, a tablespoon at a time, over the beaten egg whites. Fold in lightly.

Pour well blended mixture into a 12″ × 14″ ungreased tube pan. Bake at 350° for one hour. When finished, turn the cake upside down to cool. Frost with a butter icing if desired.

*Makes 1 large cake*

# Chocolate Angel Food Cake

Recalls a woman in her mid-fifties, "We always liked chocolate angel food cake better than white because it has more flavor." She was the family's angel-food-cake baker on noodle-making days.

¾ cup cake flour
¼ cup cocoa
¼ tsp. salt
1 tsp. cream of tartar
2 cups egg whites (14 to 16 whites)
1 tsp. vanilla
1½ cups granulated sugar

Sift flour, cocoa and salt together.

Blend the cream of tartar into the egg whites and beat them until they peak softly. Gently fold in the vanilla, then fold in the sugar, a tablespoon at a time.

Pour into an ungreased tube pan and bake at 350° for 40–45 minutes. When cake is finished, invert to cool.

*Makes 1 large cake*

# Old-Fashioned Crumb Cake

A moist coffee cake that is enhanced when eaten with applesauce, peaches or pears. It needs no icing.

3 cups flour
2 cups brown sugar
½ cup shortening, butter or margarine
1 egg, beaten
1 cup buttermilk
1 tsp. baking soda
1 tsp. cream of tartar

Mix flour and brown sugar together. Cut in shortening until mixture is crumbly. Take out 1 cup crumbs for topping.

Add to remaining crumbs the egg, buttermilk, soda and cream of tartar, in that order. Mix well after each addition.

Pour into a greased 9″ × 13″ baking pan. Sprinkle reserved cup of crumbs over top. Bake at 375° for 25–30 minutes.

*Makes 1 long cake*

# Shoofly Cake

This close kin to shoofly pie has no crust; consequently, it can be put together more quickly. The crumb topping and gooey bottom make an icing unnecessary. It is best served when slightly warm, fresh from the oven.

4 cups flour (use 2 cups whole wheat flour and 2 cups white flour, if desired)
2 cups brown sugar
1 cup butter or margarine
2 cups boiling water
1 cup molasses
2 tsp. baking soda

Work the flour, sugar and butter into fine crumbs with your fingers or a pastry mixer. Set aside 1½ cups crumbs for topping.
Mix water, molasses and baking soda together. Then add to the remaining crumbs. Mix until batter is very thin yet still lumpy.
Pour into greased and floured 9″ × 13″ cake pan. Sprinkle with reserved crumbs. Bake at 350° for 35 minutes.

*Makes 1 long cake*

# Spice Cake

This soft, gingerbread-like cake can vary slightly in its subtle flavoring by interchanging the spices used, depending upon one's own and family's preferences.

2 cups brown sugar
½ cup butter
2 eggs
1 cup sour milk
2½ cups sifted flour
1½ tsp. baking powder
1 tsp. cinnamon
1 tsp. nutmeg
1 tsp. baking soda
1 tsp. vanilla

Cream sugar and butter together until fluffy. Add eggs and beat until light.

Sift together all dry ingredients, then add them alternately with the milk to the creamed mixture, beating well after each addition. Mix in the vanilla.

Pour into greased layer pans or a 9″ × 13″ cake pan. Bake at 350° for 35–40 minutes.

*Variation:*
Use cloves instead of nutmeg.
Add 1 tsp. allspice to dry ingredients.
Add 1 tsp. cloves to dry ingredients.

*Makes 1 layer cake or 1 long cake*

# 1-2-3-4 Pound Cake

"We often baked this 1-2-3-4 cake. For a variation sometimes we would fill the last cup of flour with cocoa," remembers an 80-year-old woman who raised—and cooked for—a large family.

> 1 cup butter
> 2 cups sugar
> 3 cups cake flour (or use 2½ cups cake flour and ½ cup cocoa)
> 4 eggs
> ½ tsp. salt
> 3 tsp. baking powder
> 1 cup sour cream
> 1 tsp. vanilla

Cream butter, then add sugar gradually and beat until fluffy.
Add eggs, one by one, beating well after each addition.
Sift dry ingredients together. Mix sour cream and vanilla.
Add dry ingredients and sour cream mixture alternately to butter-sugar-egg batter, beating well continuously.
Bake in a large, greased bread pan at 350° for 1 hour.

*Makes 1 large loaf cake*

# Oatmeal Cake

A moist cake, compatible with fresh or canned fruit.

1 cup rolled oats
1¼ cups boiling water
½ cup butter or margarine
1 cup granulated sugar
1 cup brown sugar
2 eggs
1 tsp. baking soda
½ tsp. salt
1 tsp. cinnamon
1⅔ cup flour
1 tsp. vanilla

Mix oats and boiling water together; set aside for 20 minutes.

Cream butter or margarine and sugars together thoroughly. Add eggs, one at a time, beating well after each one. Blend in oatmeal mixture.

Sift together remaining dry ingredients. Fold into batter. Stir in vanilla.

Pour into a greased and floured 9″ × 13″ baking pan. Bake at 350° for 30–35 minutes.

After baking, but before the cake cools, spread the following topping over it and broil about 2 minutes or until it browns. Watch carefully since it burns easily!

*Topping*

6 Tbsp. butter or margarine, melted
¼ cup milk or cream
1 cup brown sugar
½ cup nuts, chopped

Mix together thoroughly.

*Makes 1 9″ × 13″ cake*

# Molasses Cake

Molasses was sometimes more available than sugar. A favorite topping for mush, it was a common ingredient in the pantry or cellar.

¾ cup molasses
1 egg
½ cup sour milk or buttermilk
1½ cups flour
1 tsp. baking soda
¼ cup boiling water

Combine molasses, egg and milk thoroughly. Stir in flour. Dissolve soda in boiling water, then add to batter.
Bake in a greased and floured 8″ square cake pan at 375° for 30–45 minutes.

*Makes 1 8″ square cake*

# Hickory Nut Cake

These nuts from the trees that grow wild on the fencerows flavor cakes as well as pies. The beaten egg whites (eggs were generally in good supply on the farm) make this an airy dessert.

½ cup butter or margarine, softened
1¾ cups granulated sugar
3 cups flour
3 tsp. baking powder
1 cup milk
1½ tsp. vanilla
1 cup hickory nuts
5 egg whites, beaten until stiff

Cream butter or margarine and sugar together. Mix together flour and baking powder. Add dry ingredients alternately with milk to creamed butter and sugar.
Blend in vanilla. Stir in nuts. Fold in egg whites.
Bake in 2 greased and floured cake pans at 350° for 30 minutes.

*Makes 1 layer cake*

# Rhubarb Cake

Rhubarb brings moistness and piquancy to coffee cake. This satisfies those family members and guests who prefer a hint of rhubarb rather than the full flavor of a rhubarb pie.

½ cup butter or margarine
1 cup granulated sugar
1 egg
1 tsp. vanilla
2 cups plus 2 Tbsp. flour
1 tsp. cinnamon
1 tsp. baking soda
½ tsp. salt
1 cup buttermilk or sour milk
2 cups rhubarb, finely cut
½ cup chopped nuts (optional)
½ cup grated coconut (optional)
½ cup raisins (optional)

Cream together butter or margarine and sugar. Blend in egg and vanilla.

Mix together flour, cinnamon, soda and salt. Add alternately with milk to creamed mixture.

Stir in rhubarb and any or all of the optional ingredients, mixing thoroughly.

Pour into a greased 9″ × 13″ baking pan. Bake at 350° for 45 minutes.

*Makes 1 long cake*

# Butter Cream Icing

Icings were traditionally prepared for special company or were simple additions to those cakes that seemed to need something extra. "We often ate our cakes without icing, just dusted with 10X sugar," commented a woman in her early 40s. A women ten years older explains her method, "Just beat margarine or shortening with 10X sugar and a little milk and vanilla. That's what we used to do and what I still do."

That traditional unwritten recipe has been transcribed for those who don't cook "by feel."

> 3 Tbsp. butter, margarine or shortening
> 1½ cups confectioner's sugar
> 1 Tbsp. cream or milk
> ½ tsp. vanilla

Beat shortening until smooth. Cream in (by hand or electric mixer) the sugar. When smooth add cream or milk and vanilla, beating until creamy.

*Icing for 1 long cake*

# Seven-Minute Icing

A commonly used recipe that measures the beating time — by hand — required for the icing to reach a proper consistency.

> 2 egg whites, unbeaten
> 1½ cups granulated sugar
> 5 Tbsp. cold water
> 1 tsp. light corn syrup
> 1 tsp. vanilla

Mix together egg whites, sugar, water and corn syrup in top section of double boiler. Place over rapidly boiling water and beat continuously with a rotary beater for 7 minutes. Remove from heat.

Stir in vanilla and continue beating until icing is able to be spread.

*Icing for a layer cake*

# Caramel Icing

"My mother liked a caramel icing made with brown sugar. She didn't really have a recipe." This grandmother's account is typical. Here is a written approximation of what she enjoyed on chocolate cake.

> ½ cup butter or margarine
> 1 cup brown sugar
> ¼ cup milk
> 1¾-2 cups sifted confectioner's sugar

Melt butter in saucepan. Add brown sugar and cook over low heat two minutes, stirring constantly.

Add milk and continue stirring until mixture comes to a boil.

Remove from heat and cool. Add confectioner's sugar until frosting reaches spreading consistency.

# Sour Cream Sugar Cookies

Sugar cookies' plain looks belie the emotion that sugar-cookie connoisseurs carry about them.

"Our favorites were sugar cookies with a little confectioner's sugar sprinkled on top."

"We ate lots of sugar cookies, sometimes with a little lemon in the batter."

"We made our batter with sour cream, rolled out the dough and put a raisin on top of each."

"I can't make them like my mother, who used buttermilk!"

"Drop sugar cookies are much more common than rolled-out ones."

"I make drop sugar cookies but my mother made rolled ones. Hers were spongy soft. When they're rolled and cut out, they rise to the same height all over."

Here is the first of five batters — 4 family-size batches and one crowd-size to make with visitors.

> 1½ cups sugar
> 1 cup margarine

2 eggs
1 cup sour cream or buttermilk
3¾ cups flour
2 tsp. baking powder
1 tsp. soda
1 tsp. vanilla

Cream sugar and shortening. Add eggs and beat well.
Add milk, dry ingredients and vanilla and mix thoroughly.
Drop by teaspoonful onto greased cookie sheet. Bake at
375° for 8–10 minutes.

*Variation:*
Use 1 tsp. lemon extract in place of vanilla.
Place a raisin in the center and sprinkle the top of each
cookie with sugar before baking.

# Brown Sugar Cookies

3 cups brown sugar
1 cup lard, butter or margarine, softened
2 eggs
2 tsp. baking soda
2 cups sour milk
2 tsp. baking powder
pinch of salt
5 cups flour, sifted

Cream together the brown sugar, shortening and eggs.
Stir soda into sour milk.
Sift baking powder, salt and flour together. Add milk and dry
ingredients alternately to creamed mixture.
Drop by teaspoonful onto greased cookie sheets. Bake at
350° for 7–8 minutes.

*Makes 10–11 dozen cookies*

# Drop Sugar Cookies

1 cup shortening, softened
2 cups granulated sugar
2 eggs
2 tsp. baking soda
4 tsp. baking powder
¼ tsp. salt
1 tsp. vanilla
1 cup milk
5 cups flour

Cream together shortening, sugar and eggs. Mix in baking soda and powder, salt and vanilla.
Add milk and flour alternately to creamed mixture.
Bake at 350° for 10–12 minutes.

*Makes 10–11 dozen cookies*

*Icing*

6 Tbsp. butter (at room temperature)
2 tsp. vanilla
dash of salt
1 pound confectioner's sugar, sifted
4–5 Tbsp. milk

Mix all ingredients together for 1 minute. Spread on cooled cookies, or first divide into several parts and add different food colors to each part, to give variety.

# Rolled Sour Cream Sugar Cookies

3 cups granulated sugar
1 cup lard, butter or margarine
5 eggs
2 tsp. baking soda
2 tsp. cream of tartar
1 cup sour cream
7 cups flour

Cream together the sugar, shortening and eggs.

Mix baking soda, cream of tartar and sour cream together. Add alternately with flour to the creamed mixture.

Refrigerate overnight or for seveal hours. Roll out dough and cut in desired shapes. Bake at 400° for 8–10 minutes.

*Makes about 13–15 dozen cookies*

# Sugar Cookies for a Crowd

The Amish expect unannounced company. They are seldom caught unprepared with their bountifully stocked canning shelves and flourishing gardens.

One efficient and experienced cook has found a way to both entertain and feed her guests. "I mix a big batch of sugar cookies and only bake half of them at a time. The other half I keep in the refrigerator for up to two to three weeks. What I like is if someone comes, then you have something to do. And the cookies are much better, too, when they're fresh!"

4½ cups brown sugar
2 cups lard, melted
2 cups sour cream
8 eggs
3 tsp. soda
3 tsp. cream of tartar
9 cups flour
1 Tbsp. vanilla
pinch of salt

Cream the sugar and lard. Add the sour cream and eggs and beat well. Stir in the remaining ingredients and mix well.

Drop by teaspoonsful onto greased cookie sheets. Bake at 325° for 8–10 minutes.

# Molasses Cookies

Molasses cookies, along with sugar cookies, top the list of fondly remembered old favorites. Molasses was a commonly used sweetener in the 19th century when refined sugar was at a premium in the New World.

Today's molasses cookies also call for sugar, but they retain the sturdy, cakey quality that has always made them loved.

Variations abound from household to household.

"We ate molasses spice."

"Ours were fat molasses cookies."

"We had soft molasses cakes with icing."

1 cup shortening
½ lb. light brown sugar
1 pint dark baking molasses
1 pint buttermilk
6 cups flour
1 Tbsp. baking soda

Cream shortening and sugar. Add molasses and buttermilk. Stir in flour and baking soda.

Drop in large dollops from teaspoon onto cookie sheet. Bake at 375° for 8–10 minutes.

*Variation:*

Cookies may be glazed by brushing tops with egg yolks before baking.

Add 1 tsp. ginger and 1 tsp. cinnamon with flour and soda.

*Makes 8 dozen cookies*

# Rolled Oats Cookies

"Next to molasses and sugar cookies we ate oatmeal cookies. We always bought oatmeal by the 50-pound bag."

2 cups brown sugar
1 cup lard or vegetable shortening
3 eggs

1 cup sour milk or buttermilk
1 tsp. vanilla
3 cups flour
1 tsp. baking powder
1 tsp. baking soda
1 tsp. cinnamon
½ tsp. nutmeg
½ tsp. salt
2 cups rolled oats
2 cups raisins
1 cup nuts, chopped

Cream together the sugar, shortening, eggs, milk and vanilla.
Stir dry ingredients together.
Combine dry ingredients with creamed mixture, blending thoroughly.
Drop by teaspoonsful onto greased cookie sheets. Bake at 350° for 12 – 15 minutes.

*Makes 9 dozen cookies*

# Butterscotch Cookies

2 cups brown sugar
3 eggs
1 cup shortening or lard
4 cups flour
1 tsp. baking soda
1 tsp. cream of tartar
1 cup nuts

Mix all ingredients but the nuts thoroughly in a mixer. Stir the nuts in by hand.
Roll the dough into ropes about 2 inches thick. Cut in thin slices. Cross-press with a fork to make a design.
Bake at 350° for 8 – 12 minutes.

*Makes 7 – 8 dozen cookies*

# Sour Cream Cookies

3 cups granulated sugar
1¾ cups lard or shortening
4 eggs
1 cup sour milk
1 cup sour cream
2 tsp. baking soda
4 tsp. baking powder
¾ tsp. salt
6 cups flour
1 tsp. lemon flavoring
1 Tbsp. vanilla

Cream together sugar, shortening and eggs.
Mix in remaining ingredients, combining thoroughly.
Roll out and cut in desired shapes. Sprinkle tops with granulated sugar.
Bake on greased cookie sheets at 350° for 8–10 minutes.

*Makes 12–13 dozen cookies*

# Buttermilk Cookies

2 cups brown sugar
1 cup lard or vegetable shortening
1 tsp. vanilla
2 eggs
2 tsp. baking soda
1 cup buttermilk
2 tsp. baking powder
4 cups flour
½ cup nuts, chopped (optional)

Cream together sugar and shortening. Mix in vanilla and eggs thoroughly.
Dissolve baking soda in buttermilk.
Stir baking powder into flour.
Add milk and flour mixture alternately to the creamed mixture. Stir in nuts.
Refrigerate overnight or for several hours. Drop by tea-

spoonsful onto greased cookie sheet. Bake at 400° for 8–10 minutes.

*Makes 9 dozen cookies*

# Hermits

Many varieties of dried fruit and nut cookies filled the farm pantries. Chewy and substantial, they also retained their moisture longer because of the presence of the fruit.

Here are hermits, those old-fashioned cousins of jumbies, ice box cookies, date and nut, and mincemeat cookies.

> 1 cup shortening
> 1 cup granulated sugar
> 1 cup brown sugar
> 4 eggs
> ½ cup molasses
> 1 tsp. baking soda dissolved in
>     ½ cup warm water
> 4½ cups flour
> ¼ tsp. salt
> ½ tsp. ground cloves
> 1 cup chopped nuts
> 1 cup chopped dates

Cream shortening and sugars. Add eggs and beat until light and fluffy.

Sift dry ingredients and add alternately with water and molasses. Beat after each addition.

Stir in chopped nuts and dates.

Drop by rounded teaspoons onto greased cookie sheet. Bake at 350° for 10–12 minutes.

*Variation:*

Use ½ cup cooled black coffee instead of water.

Add 1 cup raisins and 1 cup chopped dried apricots in place of nuts and dates.

*Makes about 10 dozen cookies*

# Ginger Cookies

1 cup lard, butter or margarine
1 cup granulated sugar
1 egg
2 cups dark baking molasses
2 Tbsp. vinegar
6 – 8 cups flour
¾ tsp. salt
½ tsp. cinnamon
2 Tbsp. ginger
4 tsp. baking soda
1 cup boiling water

Cream together shortening, sugar and egg. When light and fluffy beat in molasses and vinegar.

Stir together dry ingredients.

Dissolve baking soda in boiling water.

Add dry ingredients and soda-water mixture alternately to creamed ingredients. Add more flour if needed to make a soft dough.

Drop by teaspoonful onto greased cookie sheets. Sprinkle with granulated sugar. Bake at 350° for 10 minutes.

*Makes 9 – 10 dozen cookies*

# Pinwheel Date Cookies

This cookie was not part of the weekly baking; it requires far too much time in preparation! But it has traditionally been part of holiday cookie-making.

1 cup shortening
2 cups brown sugar
½ cup granulated sugar
3 eggs
4 – 4½ cups flour
1 tsp. salt
1 tsp. baking soda
1 tsp. cinnamon

Cream together the shortening and sugar. Add the eggs and beat until fluffy.

Sift the flour; then add the salt, soda and cinnamon and sift again. Add the dry ingredients to the creamed mixture and beat until smooth. Chill dough in the refrigerator for a few hours. Divide the chilled dough into two parts. Roll each ¼″ thick and spread with filling.

*Filling*

1½ cups dates or raisins, ground
1 cup sugar
1 cup water
½ cup nuts, chopped fine

Combine the fruit, sugar and water and cook until thickened, stirring constantly. Remove from heat and add the nuts. Cool and spread on the rolled dough.

Roll up, jelly-roll fashion, and chill thoroughly in the refrigerator. Slice in rings ⅛″ thick and place on greased cookie sheets, 1 inch apart. Bake at 375° until golden brown.

*Makes 3½ dozen cookies*

# Raisin Filled Cookies

1 cup lard or vegetable shortening
2 cups granulated sugar
2 eggs, beaten
1 cup milk
2 tsp. vanilla
7 cups flour
2 tsp. baking soda
2 tsp. baking powder

Cream shortening, sugar and eggs together. Blend eggs and milk. Combine with creamed mixture. Add vanilla.

Sift together dry ingredients and mix well. Stir thoroughly into batter.

Chill dough in the refrigerator for several hours or overnight. Roll to ¼" thickness on lightly floured board. Cut out with round cutter.

Place 1 teaspoon of raisin filling on the top of each of half the cookies.

With a thimble make a hole in the middle of each of the remaining cookies (the hole will prevent the filling from cooking out between the cookie halves). Place these cookies on top of the cookies with filling. Do not press together.

Bake at 350° for 20 minutes on greased cookie sheets.

*Filling*

2 cups raisins, chopped or ground
1 cup sugar
1 cup water
2 Tbsp. flour
1 Tbsp. lemon juice (optional)

Combine all ingredients and bring to a boil, stirring constantly until thickened.

*Makes 5–6 dozen cookies*

# Sand Tarts

Although Christmas is celebrated quietly, some families have kept a few cooking traditions, especially to honor visitors over the holidays.

At the turn of the century, sand tarts were baked in some homes "at Christmastime, and usually only then. We would cut them out in different shapes," an elderly woman remarks. The traditional Pennsylvania Dutch Cookies — lebkuchen, pefferniss and springerle — were not commonly eaten by the Amish. Explained an Amish grandfather, "We had more cookies around at Christmas, but not really special kinds."

Today cookie-baking is associated more with holiday activity, and sand tarts continue as favorites, perhaps because children enjoy both cutting them out and choosing special shapes to eat.

    1 cup butter
    2 cups granulated sugar
    3 eggs
    1 tsp. vanilla
    1 tsp. salt
    2 tsp. baking powder
    3½ – 4 cups flour

Cream together butter and sugar. Add eggs and vanilla and beat until fluffy.

Mix dry ingredients together and beat into batter until a soft dough forms. Refrigerate several hours or overnight.

Roll dough very thin and cut in decorative shapes with cookie cutters. Brush tops of cookies with egg whites and sprinkle with colored sugar and crushed peanuts, walnuts or pecans.

Bake at 350° for 8 – 10 minutes on greased cookie sheets.

*Makes 4 – 5 dozen cookies*

# Whoopie Pies

These cookies are a relatively new invention, first appearing about 30–35 years ago. Said one grandmother in her mid-50s, "I don't remember whoopie pies as a little girl, but I do know they were around before we were married. Probably someone just made them up!"

Another grandmother in her late 50s knew of them "just since we're married, and that not in the first years."

These individual cakes are well suited to lunch-box travel and food stands at farm sales. The icing is spread between the two cookie halves so it doesn't rub off when wrapped, as cupcake icing does.

The original — and still most commonly made — whoopie pie is chocolate. Oatmeal and pumpkin variations have developed more recently.

    2 cups sugar
    1 cup shortening
    2 eggs
    4 cups flour
    1 cup baking cocoa
    2 tsp. vanilla
    1 tsp. salt
    1 cup sour milk
    2 tsp. baking soda
    1 cup hot water

Cream sugar and shortening. Add eggs.

Sift together flour, cocoa and salt. Add to creamed mixture alternately with sour milk. Add vanilla.

Dissolve soda in hot water and add last. Mix well.

Drop by rounded teaspoonsful onto cookie sheet. Bake at 400° for 8–10 minutes.

Make sandwiches from 2 cookies filled with Whoopie Pie Filling.

*Makes 4 dozen sandwich pies*

Chicken Corn Soup (page 40)

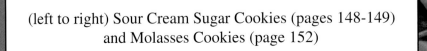

(left to right) Sour Cream Sugar Cookies (pages 148-149)
and Molasses Cookies (page 152)

*Filling*

2 egg whites, beaten
4 Tbsp. milk
2 tsp. vanilla
4 cups 10X sugar
1½ cups shortening

Mix together egg whites, milk, vanilla and 2 cups 10X sugar. Then beat in shortening and remaining 2 cups of 10X sugar.

Spread dab of filling on flat side of cooled cookie. Top with another cookie to form a sandwich pie.

# Oatmeal Whoopie Pies

2 cups brown sugar
¾ cup butter or shortening
2 eggs
½ tsp. salt
1 tsp. cinnamon
1 tsp. baking powder
3 Tbsp. boiling water
1 tsp. soda
2½ cups flour
2 cups oatmeal

Cream sugar and shortening. Add eggs; then add salt, cinnamon and baking powder.

Add soda dissolved in hot water. Gradually add flour and oatmeal.

Drop batter by heaping teaspoons onto greased cookie sheet. Bake at 350° for 8–10 minutes or until brown.

Use ½ Whoopie Pie Filling recipe above to fill sandwich pies.

*Makes 3 dozen sandwich pies*

# Pumpkin Whoopie Pies

2 cups brown sugar
1 cup vegetable oil
1½ cups cooked, mashed pumpkin
2 eggs
3 cups flour
1 tsp. salt
1 tsp. baking powder
1 tsp. baking soda
1 tsp. vanilla
1½ Tbsp. cinnamon
½ Tbsp. ginger
½ Tbsp. ground cloves

Cream sugar and oil.

Add pumpkin and eggs. Add flour, salt, baking powder, soda, vanilla and spices. Mix well.

Drop by heaping teaspoons onto greased cookie sheet. Bake at 350° for 10–12 minutes.

Make sandwiches from 2 cookies filled with ½ the Whoopie Pie Filling recipe on page 161.

*Variation:*

Adding ½ cup black walnuts (ground) gives these cookies a special delicious flavor.

*Makes 3 dozen sandwich pies*

# Puddings, Dumplings and Desserts

The Amish, as a whole, work hard and lead disciplined, restrained lives. Yet they relish good food and indulge in desserts, almost with abandon. While pie will probably never be surpassed as a favorite, it has strong competitors — cracker pudding, stewed rhubarb and apple dumplings are all highly regarded!

A cook responsible for three full meals a day wants to broaden her menu, prepare food that's enjoyable and fill up the folks. So whether it's a soup-and-sandwich lunch or a full meat-and-potatoes dinner, there's bound to be a dessert of substance.

Certain of these dishes make a meal, reflecting their history and the fondness with which they are held. Apple roll, for example, with its dumpling-like dough, likely evolved from the traditional boiled puddings, commonly eaten in early Pennsylvania, in bowls of milk.[7] Cornstarch pudding, known as "pap," also formed the basis of many snack-meals.

Many of these dishes are flavored with fruit or easily available extracts, such as vanilla. Others are built around crackers, those near-essentials in the Amish diet. Eggs and milk are usually present, either in the mix itself or at least in the eating.

These traditional specialties stand alone as dessert for daily family meals. When there is company at the table they are usually served as accompaniments to pie and cake.

# Vanilla Cornstarch Pudding

"Mom made a lot of cornstarch pudding," recounts a young mother. "She would make it for Sunday lunch, especially if company was coming, and we would eat it warm. Often we would spread crackers with peanut butter and dunk them in it."

The most typical flavor was vanilla, but some cooks delighted their families by putting a dollop of chocolate right in the center of the full serving dish. "Mom would save a little pudding out, mix it with chocolate syrup, then spoon it back into the middle to give it all a little more flavor," remembers a middle-aged woman.

Preferences vary as to the proper temperature at which cornstarch should be served. Some insist on having it warm. Others are equally adamant about eating it cold. In cases where the batch is larger than the call for it, the first round is served hot; the leftovers are chilled.

> 1 quart fresh milk
> ⅔ cup granulated sugar
> ⅓ cup cornstarch
> dash of salt
> 2 eggs, beaten
> ¼ cup milk
> 1 tsp. vanilla

Scald 1 quart milk in top of double boiler. Meanwhile, combine the sugar, cornstarch, salt, eggs and ¼ cup milk. When smooth, add to the scalded milk and cook, stirring constantly, until thickened.

Remove from heat and stir in vanilla.

*Makes 8 – 10 servings*

# Chocolate Cornstarch Pudding

> 3 Tbsp. cornstarch
> ⅓ cup sugar
> ½ tsp. salt
> 3 Tbsp. cocoa
> 2 cups milk
> 1 tsp. vanilla

Mix dry ingredients well. In a saucepan heat 1½ cups milk. Add other ½ cup milk to the dry ingredients and stir until smooth.

When the milk is hot, but before a skin forms, stir in the dampened dry ingredients. Stir constantly over heat until the mixture thickens and comes to a gentle boil (it should not boil vigorously). Remove from heat and serve either warm or cold.

*Makes 4 – 6 servings*

# Cracker Pudding

Cracker pudding at mealtime was a pleasurable routine. It is one more way to include saltines in the diet, although their presence is scarcely distinguishable in the finished dessert.

Even 75 years ago the Amish of eastern Pennsylvania had access to coconuts. "We would buy a whole one and grate it ourselves," says an 80-plus-year-old.

> **2 eggs, separated**
> **⅔ cup granulated sugar**
> **1 quart milk**
> **1¼-1½ cups saltine crackers, coarsely broken**
> **¾ cup coconut, grated (optional)**
> **1 tsp. vanilla**
> **3 Tbsp. sugar**

Beat egg yolks and sugar together. Pour into saucepan and heat. Gradually add the milk, stirring constantly.

Add crackers and coconut and cook until thickened. Remove from heat and stir in vanilla.

Pour into baking dish. Add 3 Tbsp. sugar to egg whites and beat until stiffened. Spread over pudding, then brown the meringue under the broiler.

*Variation:*

Beat the egg whites until stiff, then fold them into the pudding while it is still hot.

Chill and serve.

*Makes 6 – 8 servings*

# Graham Cracker Pudding

A pudding of special delight to children!

16 whole graham crackers
¼ cup granulated sugar
¼ cup butter or margarine, melted
4 tsp. flour
½ cup plus 2 Tbsp. sugar
2 cups milk
3 eggs, separated
½ tsp. vanilla

Crush graham crackers. Combine with ¼ cup sugar and butter. Mix to form fine crumbs. Press ¾ of crumb mixture into bottom and sides of baking dish. Reserve remaining crumbs.

Combine flour and ½ cup sugar in top of double boiler. Add milk. Heat to boiling. Beat egg yolks and combine with ½ cup of the hot milk mixture. Pour back into the remaining hot milk and heat to boiling again. Boil 2–3 minutes, stirring constantly. Remove from heat and add vanilla. Pour into cracker-lined dish.

Beat egg whites until stiff. Gradually add remaining 2 Tbsp. sugar. Pile beaten egg whites on top of pudding. Sprinkle with reserved cracker crumbs. Bake at 350° for 5–8 minutes until meringue is browned. Cool before serving.

*Makes 8–10 servings*

# Banana Pudding

Prepare Graham Cracker Pudding above. Pour one-third of custard into cracker-lined dish. Top with sliced bananas. Continue alternating layers of pudding and bananas. End with meringue and a sprinkling of reserved cracker crumbs.

*Makes 8–10 servings*

# Tapioca Pudding

Years ago, the preparation of tapioca pudding was not a last-minute inspiration. "We used the big pearl tapioca that had to soak overnight," explains one elderly woman. Despite that, "we ate a lot of tapioca pudding," says another.

> 4 cups milk
> 1/3 cup minute tapioca
> 2 eggs, separated
> 1/2 cup sugar
> pinch of salt
> 1/2 tsp. vanilla or lemon extract

Combine milk and tapioca in heavy saucepan. Cook, stirring constantly, until tapioca is clear.

Beat egg yolks with sugar and salt. Add 1/2 cup hot milk mixture to egg yolks. Return this to remaining hot milk. Heat again to boiling point. Boil 2 minutes, stirring constantly. Remove from heat.

Fold in stiffly beaten egg whites and flavoring. Pour into serving dish.

*Makes about 10 servings*

# Apple Dumplings

These individually packaged apple "pies" make a meal or a monumental dessert. They are best eaten warm with cold milk poured over.

 8 apples, cored and pared
 3 cups flour
 1 tsp. salt
 1¼ cups shortening
 1 egg, beaten
 ⅓ cup cold water
 1 Tbsp. vinegar
 ½ cup margarine
 1 cup brown sugar
 4 Tbsp. water

Mix flour and salt. Cut in shortening.

Combine egg, ⅓ cup cold water and vinegar and stir into the shortening mixture. Let stand a few minutes.

Roll out dough on floured board and cut into squares, so that each is large enough to fit up around an apple. When an apple is completely wrapped in dough, place it in a greased 9″ × 13″ baking pan.

Bring margarine, brown sugar and 4 Tbsp. water to a boil. Pour over dumplings.

Bake at 350° for 40–50 minutes or until dumplings are golden brown.

*Makes 8 servings*

# Apple Rolls

This variation on apple dumplings was served as a main meal or a lighter supper. "We sometimes ate it with potatoes to make it more substantial," remembers a young Amish mother. "It's like a fruity cinnamon roll."

4 cups flour
2 Tbsp. granulated sugar
2 Tbsp. baking powder
1 tsp. salt
2½ Tbsp. shortening
1 egg
milk
6 medium-sized apples, peeled, cored and sliced

Combine dry ingredients. Cut in shortening until mixture resembles small peas.

Beat egg in cup, then fill the cup with milk. Mix into crumbs until dough forms.

Roll out to ¼" thickness. Cover with sliced apples. Roll up, like a jelly roll, and cut in 1" slices. Lay in greased baking pan, pour hot syrup over and bake at 375° for 35–40 minutes. Serve warm with milk.

*Makes 6–8 servings*

*Syrup*

2 cups brown sugar
2 cups water
¼ cup butter or margarine
2 Tbsp. flour

Mix together. Bring to a boil, stirring until smooth. Simmer for 3 minutes. Pour over apple rolls.

# Baked Apples

Lighter than dumplings or a cobbler, yet dessert-like. Eat warm from the oven—plain or with milk, whipped cream or ice cream.

These apples also complement mush and eggs, scrapple and fried potatoes.

8–10 apples, cored, peeled and cut in half
¾ cup granulated sugar
¾ cup brown sugar
½ cup flour
1 tsp. cinnamon
2 tsp. butter or margarine, melted
1 cup water

Place apples in a greased 9″ × 13″ baking pan.

Mix remaining ingredients together in order in a saucepan and bring to a boil. Simmer, stirring, until thickened.

Pour syrup over apples and bake at 350° for 30–45 minutes or until apples are tender.

*Makes 8–10 servings*

# Baked Egg Custard

6 eggs
6 Tbsp. sugar
dash of salt
1 Tbsp. vanilla
1 quart milk

Beat eggs, then stir in sugar, salt and vanilla.

Scald milk and gradually add it to the egg mixture. Stir until it is thoroughly blended.

Pour into custard cups or a baking pan. Set in a pan of hot water that is a height equal to the level of the custard.

Bake at 325° for 40 minutes or until a knife inserted in the center of the custard comes out clean.

*Makes 8 servings*

# Caramel Pudding

One older woman remembers that her grandmother served this for supper on the day her family hosted the church service.

"Grussmommy never knew how many people she'd have, but she usually made caramel pudding! I love it with ground peanuts on top. I can still see Dauddy sitting there, shelling the peanuts for on top. Grussmommy always served it cold."

2 Tbsp. butter
¾ cup brown sugar
1 quart milk
2 eggs
2 Tbsp. cornstarch
2 Tbsp. flour
pinch of salt
¼ cup milk
chopped peanuts

Melt the butter in a heavy saucepan. Add the brown sugar and stir until brown. Stir in 1 quart milk and warm; then set aside.

Beat together eggs, cornstarch, flour, salt and ¼ cup milk. Add to the warm milk and stir just until it reaches the boiling point. Remove from heat and beat with a rotary beater. Cool; then cover top with chopped fresh peanuts before serving.

*Makes 8 servings*

# Glorified Rice

More familiar among the Amish than traditional rice pudding, this variety called for a bought fruit that cast the whole dish into the category of a special treat. Cooks frequently planned for this dessert by making more rice as a vegetable than could be eaten at one meal.

>   2 cups cooked rice
>   ½ cup sugar
>   1 cup pineapple chunks, drained
>   1 cup whipping cream

Combine rice, sugar and pineapple chunks. Refrigerate for at least one hour.

Just before serving, whip cream and fold into rice mixture.

*Makes 6 servings*

# Apple Crisp

Apples, so abundant and versatile, have stayed on the Amish menu consistently through the years. What has changed are the batters and mixtures that surround the fruit. Cobblers and crunches are modified puddings and dumplings, developed because of the availability of different ingredients and the people's interest in eating lighter foods.

>   ¾ cup granulated sugar
>   1 Tbsp. flour
>   ½ tsp. cinnamon
>   ⅛ tsp. salt
>   2 cups apples, cored, peeled and sliced
>   ½ cup oatmeal
>   ½ cup flour
>   ½ cup brown sugar
>   ⅛ tsp. baking soda
>   ⅛ tsp. baking powder
>   ¼ cup butter or margarine, melted

Sift together granulated sugar, 1 Tbsp. flour, cinnamon and salt. Gently combine with apple slices. Spoon into greased 8″ × 12″ baking pan.

Mix together well the oatmeal, ½ cup flour, brown sugar, baking soda and powder. Stir in melted shortening. Crumble over apple mixture.

Bake at 375° for 35 – 40 minutes. Serve warm or cold with milk.

*Makes 6 – 8 servings*

# Rhubarb Sauce

This tangy fruit dish works equally well as a main meal salad (it can substitute for applesauce and chow-chow) or dessert.

Debates can develop over whether it is best with the addition of strawberries or orange rind!

1 quart fresh rhubarb, sliced thin
water
2½ Tbsp. granulated tapioca
¾ cup granulated sugar
2 cups fresh strawberries, sliced (optional)
1½ Tbsp. grated orange rind (optional)

Place cut-up rhubarb in saucepan. Add water to cover half the rhubarb. Stir in tapioca and sugar, mixing well. Let stand 30 minutes. Add strawberries, if desired.

Cover pan and bring fruit to boil. Cook until rhubarb is tender but not mushy.

Remove from heat and add orange rind, if desired, and soda. (Soda will cause rhubarb to foam up momentarily.) Chill and serve.

*Makes 6 – 8 servings*

# Rhubarb Crumble

Rhubarb Pot Pie could weigh heavily in one's stomach for the better part of a day: "Melt and brown butter in a kettle. Put in a layer of dough, then a layer of cooked rhubarb and sugar. Repeat until you have as much as wanted. Be sure to have dough on top. Cover the kettle and bake ½–¾ hour on not too hot a stove." That dish was designed for a busy cook—and consumers who exercised vigorously.

One adaptation of this rhubarb dessert has more crunch and sits more lightly—Rhubarb Crumble.

> 1 cup flour, sifted (½ white; ½ whole wheat)
> ¼ cup oatmeal, uncooked
> 1 cup brown sugar, packed
> ½ cup butter, melted
> 1 tsp. cinnamon
> 1 cup granulated sugar
> 2 Tbsp. cornstarch
> 1 cup water
> 1 tsp. vanilla
> 2 cups rhubarb, diced

Stir together flour, oatmeal, brown sugar, butter and cinnamon until crumbly. Set aside half of crumbs. Pat remaining crumbs over bottom of 9″ square baking pan.

Combine sugar, cornstarch, water and vanilla, stirring until smooth. Add rhubarb and cook until mixture becomes thick and clear.

Pour rhubarb sauce over crumbs. Crumble remaining crumbs over top sauce.
Bake at 350° for 1 hour.

*Variation:*
Use cherries or blueberries instead of rhubarb.

*Makes 6–8 servings*

# Rhubarb Dumplings

2 cups rhubarb
2 cups flour
1 tsp. salt
2 tsp. baking powder
3 Tbsp. butter, margarine or lard
¾ cup plus 2 Tbsp. milk
butter or margarine, softened
granulated sugar
nutmeg

Cut rhubarb into ¼" slices and set aside.

Sift flour, salt and baking powder together. Cut the shortening into the dry ingredients until mixture resembles small peas. Stir in the milk, blending thoroughly.

Roll dough out to ¼" thickness, then spread it with butter. Sprinkle sugar over. Cover with rhubarb slices and dust with nutmeg.

Roll dough up in jelly-roll fashion. Cut into slices 1½–2" thick. Lay slices flat in a baking pan and pour sweet sauce over. Bake at 350° for 45 minutes or until golden brown.

*Makes 6–8 servings*

*Sweet Sauce*

1 cup granulated sugar
1½ Tbsp. flour
¼ tsp. salt
1 cup hot water
1½ Tbsp. butter or margarine

Mix all ingredients together until smooth. Bring to boil, then cook for 3 minutes, stirring constantly.

# Grape Mush

Certain treats are the by-product of occasional cooking operations. Grape-juice making is one such event; it leaves behind a thick and tasty pulp, too flavorful to ignore or dispose of.

After the clear juice has drained out of the boiled grapes, the "mush" that is left can be put through a press to separate out the seeds and skins.

As one experienced cook explains, "Add cornstarch or tapioca to the hot mush, plus sugar to taste. Cook until it thickens slightly. Let it cool and eat it. That is a dessert!"

# Raspberries with Knepp

2 cups raspberries
¾ cup granulated sugar
2 cups water
3 Tbsp. cornstarch
⅓ cup water
¾ cup flour
5 tsp. baking powder
3 tsp. granulated sugar
dash of salt
1 cup milk

Gently mix raspberries, ¾ cup sugar and 2 cups water together in a saucepan and bring to a boil.

Dissolve cornstarch in ⅓ cup water, then stir into boiling raspberry mixture. Stir until thickened.

Stir flour, baking powder, sugar and salt together. Add milk and stir until smooth.

Drop that batter by teaspoonful into the boiling raspberries. Cover tightly and let simmer for 20 minutes without lifting the lid.

Serve warm with milk.

*Makes 8 – 10 servings*

# Corn Pone

"Mother made a kind of shortcake with cornmeal. We ate it hot, always with cherries and milk, for our snack meal or on Saturdays at dinnertime," explains a woman born in the 1920s.

One more use for the home-dried, mill-ground cornmeal.

1 cup sugar
½ cup butter or shortening, softened
2 eggs
1½ cups cornmeal
1½ cups flour
3 tsp. baking powder
½ tsp. salt
1½ cups milk

Cream sugar and shortening. Add eggs and beat well. Combine cornmeal, flour, baking powder and salt. Add alternately with milk.

Pour into a greased and floured 9″ × 13″ cake pan or two round layer cake pans. Bake at 350° for 45 minutes.

*Fills one 9″ × 13″ pan*

# Cottage Pudding

This cake bears a name tying it to those cakey puddings that in 19th century America were steamed or boiled and often eaten with fruit and milk.

Today it could fit into the shortcake family.

¼ cup butter, margarine or shortening
⅔ cup granulated sugar
1 egg, well beaten
1 tsp. vanilla
2½ cups flour
4 tsp. baking powder
½ tsp. salt
1 cup milk

Cream shortening and sugar together. Beat in egg and vanilla until fluffy.

Sift dry ingredients together and then add alternately with the milk to the creamed batter. Do not over-stir.

Bake in a greased 8″ square cake pan at 350° for 35 minutes. Serve with fruit and milk.

*Makes 8 servings*

# Date Pudding

This moist, rich dessert is more commonly eaten in the Ohio Amish communities than in the Pennsylvania ones. The settlements further west likely learned it from their neighbors. The cake's base of dried fruit makes it appealing to the Amish who enjoy that chewy sweetness.

    1 cup boiling water
    1 cup dates, cut up
    ½ cup granulated sugar
    ½ cup brown sugar
    1 egg
    2 Tbsp. butter or margarine, softened
    1½ cups flour
    1 tsp. baking powder
    1 tsp. baking soda
    ½ tsp. salt
    1 cup nuts, chopped

Pour boiling water over dates and set aside to cool.
Cream together sugars, egg and butter or margarine.
Combine dry ingredients and blend into creamed batter. Stir in dates and nuts.
Pour into a greased baking pan, 11″ × 7″ × 1½″. Top with sauce and bake at 350° for 40–45 minutes. Serve warm or cold, topped with whipped cream, if desired.

*Makes 6–8 servings*

*Sauce*

    1½ cups brown sugar
    1 Tbsp. butter or margarine, melted
    1½ cups boiling water

Mix together until smooth and syrupy. Pour over batter and bake.

# Homemade Ice Cream

Homemade ice cream was a rare treat. A hand-cranked freezer was an appropriate wedding gift, so many families had one in the cellar, attic or kettlehouse.

For those without a freezer or the time to prepare the mix and turn it, there was another alternative. "Mother made snow ice cream. We had an old freezer but we seldom used it," remembers a woman in her mid-50s.

Another recalls, "We always made ice cream in the winter when we had ice! We used a cornstarch pudding, cooked base. Then we'd sit up to the cookstove with our feet propped up on it to stay warm!"

> 1 gallon rich milk
> 4 cups granulated sugar
> ¾ tsp. salt
> 2 Tbsp. flour
> 2 Tbsp. cornstarch
> 4 eggs, beaten
> ½ cup cream
> 1 Tbsp. vanilla

Heat the milk, sugar and salt together.

Meanwhile, mix the flour, cornstarch, eggs and cream together until smooth. Stir in hot milk, return to the stove, and bring to a boil, stirring constantly until thickened.

Remove from heat and add vanilla. Let cool, then process according to freezer's instructions.

*Makes 6 quarts ice cream*

# Fruit Butters, Jellies and Jams

Fruity spreads, jams and jellies balanced the rich meat-gravy-potato-noodle menus served at Pennsylvania German tables. In the mid-19th century these toppings had a more tart than sweet flavor and in some cases were prepared with a decidedly sour syrup.

In time, the German settlers learned a preference for sweetened preserves from their English neighbors. That shift in tastes occurred as beef came to be eaten more regularly and as sugar became available in a more refined form. A trend toward the increased use of sugar was happening generally throughout America during the 1860s.[8]

Bountiful gardens and orchards produce more than a family can eat in season. Jams and jellies have always preserved those fruits and flavors far past the growing months. And in a setting where bread is a fixture in the diet, these spreads disappear quickly, often teamed with schmierkase, molasses or peanut butter.

In years gone by, jams, jellies and fruit butters were boiled with sugar until they reached a spreadable consistency. With the advent of Certo® and later Sure-Jell® and gelatin, some efficiency-minded Amish cooks adopted the convenience those products offer.

One grandmother remembers her mother marrying old and new techniques in her preparation of peach jelly. "She would peel and seed the fruit, canning jars and jars of peaches. But the skins and seeds she would save and boil to extract the flavor in a good juice. To that she would add Certo® or Sure-Jell® for thickening.'' Although the woman was economically inclined, she did treat herself, her family and guests to a special occasional treat. ''My mother liked pineapple jelly. That was her company jelly. She would buy fresh pineapples to make it.''

Although defensibly a bid against wasting ripened fruits, jams and jellies were—and still are—a place for an Amish cook to show a bit of flourish.

# Apple Butter

Today apple butter is considered a credit to the Pennsylvania German food tradition. Historically, however, it was sweetened only lightly, if at all, making it a spread children avoided rather than relished. One middle-aged woman remembers, "An apple butter sandwich was not considered a treat!" Pear butter was much preferred, "because it was sweet and more mild compared to apple butter, yet not all that flavorful either."

Varieties of fruit butters and preserves were regarded as medicines in Germany and likely influenced their handling in the New World. But with the increased influence of the neighboring English and the easier availability of refined sugar, apple butter grew in favor.

Years ago, apple-butter making was an all-day affair. Generally it was an intergenerational family event. Here is one adaptation of such a day that requires a lot of outdoor space for production and substantial indoor storage for the finished spread.

> 40 gallons apple cider
> 40 bushels apples
> 40 lbs. granulated sugar

Heat cider to boiling at 5:30 a.m.

Peel, core and slice apples. At 2:30 p.m. add ⅓ of the apple slices. After this addition the mixture must be stirred constantly.

At 3:30 p.m. add another ⅓ of the apples. Add sugar gradually.

At 4:30 p.m. add the remaining apples.

Continue stirring mixture until about 8:00 p.m. or until apple butter is thickened. Pour into jars and seal.

*Makes 25 gallons*

# Apple Butter in the Oven

This is, admittedly, a short-cut procedure that fits better in smaller kitchens and homesteads than the outdoor apple-butter business demands.

One woman, who grew up helping to stir the cider for hours as it boiled down, discovered this method after much experimenting.

**8 quarts thick applesauce**
**8 quarts fresh cider**
**4 cups brown sugar**
**1 tsp. salt**

Make 8 quarts of thick applesauce. Place hot applesauce into the oven at 400°.

Place cider in large kettle and boil until half has evaporated. Add cider to sauce in the oven. Allow oven door to stand slightly ajar so steam can escape. Stir occasionally.

After about 2 hours add sugar and salt. Mix well. Allow about 2 more hours of cooking time until apple butter is the desired consistency, remembering to stir occasionally. Seal in jars.

# Pear Butter

"Grussmommy would come the night before and we'd all peel pears. Baskets of them," one woman remembers. "Then the next morning Dauddy would bring Grussmommy over while those pears started cooking in our big copper kettle. We had a big wooden paddle to stir with, so the pears wouldn't scorch.

"When the pears got soft we put them through the fruit press." That smoothed the sauce. "Then we poured it back into the copper kettle and added 100 pounds of sugar. The sauce just boiled for hours. Somebody had to stir it constantly or it would burn. When it had boiled down, Grussmommy would test it with a spoon to see if it had reached a jelly-like consistency."

It was the moment for a skilled judgment. If Grussmommy decided it was right, into the crocks it went. The line-up of crocks had all been warmed—quarts, two-quarts and gallons. "After they were filled we took bread wrappers, cut them to fit the tops of the crocks, dipped the wrappers in water, then put them down on top of the butter. We didn't have waxed paper then.''

The butter was doubly sealed. "Next we took newspapers or brown paper and fit it down over the tops and outsides of the crocks. Then we cut rubber bands from inner tubes and tied them tightly around the paper. That pear butter would keep for a whole year. It didn't get moldy and biting.''

Here is a version more suitable for today's schedule and living space.

    6 quarts pear sauce
    1 quart apple cider
    ¼ tsp. cinnamon
    3 lbs. brown sugar

To make pear sauce, wash, core and peel pears. Cut into quarters. Add a little water and cook until soft and mushy.

Mix pear sauce with cider, cinnamon and brown sugar in large roaster. Place in a 400° oven for 3–4 hours. Stir occasionally during baking time. Allow oven door to stand a bit ajar so moisture can escape. This will boil down to about ½ volume. Put in jars and seal.

# Strawberry Jam

    1 quart strawberries
    2 cups granulated sugar
    2 cups granulated sugar
    2 tsp. lemon juice

Stir strawberries and 2 cups sugar together. Bring to boil and simmer for 5 minutes, stirring frequently. Stir in 2 more cups sugar and lemon juice. Bring to boil and continue boiling for 10 more minutes, stirring frequently.

Let stand for 24 hours. Spoon into jars and seal.

# Rhubarb Jam

**3 lbs. rhubarb**
**½ cup water**
**4 cups granulated sugar**
**2 oranges**

Remove papery skin from rhubarb, then cut into ½″ pieces. Place in saucepan with water, sugar, zest of oranges and juice squeezed from oranges.

Bring to boil. Simmer for 30 minutes, stirring constantly.

Pour into jars and seal.

# Grape Butter

**1 quart grapes, washed and drained**
**4 cups granulated sugar**
**¼ cup water**

Mix together, bring to boil and cook for 20 minutes, stirring frequently. Put through food press. Pour into pint jars and seal.

*Makes about 2 pints of jam*

# Peach Preserves

**2 quarts peeled and sliced ripe peaches**
**6 cups granulated sugar**

Stir fruit and sugar together. Let stand in cool place for 12–18 hours.

Bring to boil, stirring often. Let simmer until fruit thickens and becomes clear, about 40 minutes. Continue to stir throughout cooking time.

Spoon into jars and seal.

# Raspberry Jelly

1 quart raspberries
water
2 cups granulated sugar
2 Tbsp. cider vinegar
½ tsp. cream of tartar

Place raspberries in saucepan and cover with water. Bring to boil, then simmer slowly, uncovered, until fruit is tender.

Pour into a cloth bag, suspended over a bowl or dishpan, and let drain without squeezing the bag (to allow juice to remain clear).

Return juice to saucepan (should be about 2 cups) and stir in vinegar and cream of tartar (adjust amounts if juice quantity is different).

Bring to boil and continue cooking on high until jelly thickens.

Pour into jars and seal.

# Blackberry Jelly

2 quarts blackberries
3 cups water
granulated sugar

Place washed and drained blackberries and water in saucepan. Bring to boil and cook until soft.

Pour cooked berries into cloth bag and allow to drain (do not squeeze bag so that juice remains clear).

Measure juice and return to saucepan. Add sugar, equal to the amount of juice, and bring to boil. Cook on high until jelly thickens.

Pour into jars and seal.

# Elderberry Jelly

1 quart elderberries
water
granulated sugar

Pour berries into saucepan. Cover with water. Bring to boil and continue cooking until berries are soft. Pour into cloth bag, suspended over a bowl or dishpan, and allow to drain (do not squeeze bag so the juice remains clear).

Measure juice and return to saucepan. Add an equal amount of sugar, stir and bring to a boil. Cook quickly until jelly thickens.

Pour into jars and seal.

# Pineapple Jam

4 cups fresh pineapple
4 cups water
4 cups granulated sugar

Cut pineapple into small chunks. Put into saucepan, add water and cook until tender.

Stir in sugar and continue cooking until fruit thickens and is clear.

Pour into jars and seal.

# Tomato Jam

**3 pounds (about 6 large) ripe tomatoes**
**1 lemon, sliced thin**
**5 cups granulated sugar**

Skin, core and quarter tomatoes. Remove seeds. Put tomatoes in saucepan and bring to boil. Simmer, uncovered, for 8–10 minutes. This should yield about 3 cups pulp (adjust other ingredients accordingly if it varies from this).

Return tomatoes to pan. Stir in lemon slices and sugar. Bring to boil and continue cooking, stirring constantly until jam thickens.

Pour into jars and seal.

# Church Spread

Bread is customarily a prime ingredient at the lunch following the Old Order Amish Sunday church service. What is offered as a topping for it has changed over time and continues to vary depending upon the district and individual hosting home.

Schmierkase, apple butter and jams and jellies in manifold combinations have all been popular.

**1 gallon light corn syrup or molasses**
**1 gallon marshmallow cream**
**2½ lbs. peanut butter (chunky or smooth) or grape or**
    **strawberry jelly**

Mix together well until creamy and spreadable.

# Cheese

Cheese-making came naturally on early Pennsylvania farms. Most families had a few cows for their own dairy supplies. What milk they didn't use for drinking they mixed into cake and cookie batters. But when the sour milk got ahead of the demand, the cook made cheese. She drew upon a tradition learned in Europe; in this country she made schmierkase, egg cheese, ball cheese and cup cheese.

When dairying increased in eastern Pennsylvania, there were still regular occasions when there was milk for cheese-making. An elderly woman recalls, "When we were first on the farm, the milk company that we sold to didn't haul milk on Sundays. In the summer we couldn't ship that milk so we'd have several milk cans full and I'd make cheese from that. I made it mostly for our family."

Along the way, schmierkase began to be served at Sunday lunch following the church service. Cheese spread was frequently more plentiful than jam or jelly. "It's not something we always ate at church. If the cows went dry we couldn't have it!" But it became a rather regular feature on the Sunday lunch menu.

Change keeps altering what was once routine, however, even in the Amish community. "There is a problem, now, with getting the crumbs to make the cheese," explained a young Amish woman. The reason? "I don't know Amish people who have just a few cows now. Either they have a dairy and ship all their milk, or they have just one cow and don't get enough milk to sour for cheese. I get all my curds from a Mennonite lady whose family does have a few cows. She makes crumbs from the excess milk they don't use."

A local store or two sells the cheese crumbs, but the Amish, who have a tradition of producing their own, think the price is a bit high. So they make adjustments. "For church we melt the processed orange American cheese with some margarine, evaporated milk and regular milk. It really tastes almost like the old schmier-kase," offered a middle-aged woman. An older man commented that in the church district of which he is a member, "We almost always have peanut butter mixed with margarine and something creamy like marshmallow. It spreads easily; it's not too rich."

Here are recipes for four old favorites, despite the fact that today they are only rarely on the cook's agenda.

Ham and Green Beans (page 19)

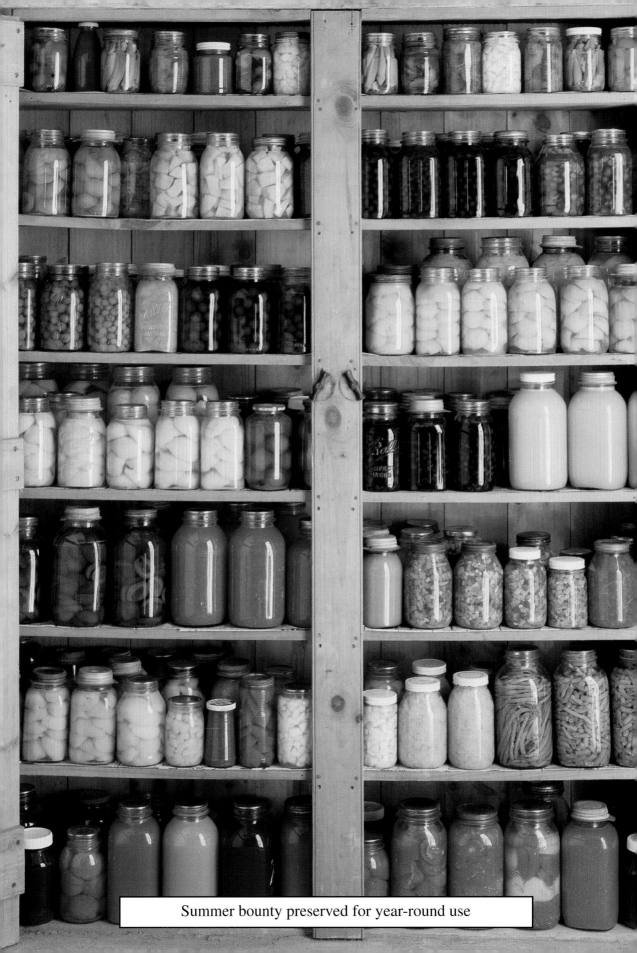

Summer bounty preserved for year-round use

# Schmierkase

2½ gallons milk, skimmed of its cream
2 tsp. baking soda
1¼ – 1½ cups warm water
⅓ cup butter
2 tsp. salt
1 cup hot water

Let milk sour until it becomes very thick, then heat to 115° – 120°.

Pour half of milk into a coarse cloth bag to drain. Squeeze out as much liquid as possible. Empty curds into a bowl and crumble. Repeat process with remaining milk.

Let crumbs set at room temperature for 2 to 3 days (up to 5 days if a stronger flavor is desired).

To crumbs (should be about 4 cups) add baking soda and mix well. Pour into double boiler and let stand for 30 minutes, then add 1¼ – 1½ cups warm water.

Bring to boil, stirring constantly. Mix in butter and salt and finally the cup of hot water, adding it ¼ cup at a time.

Cook for 10 – 12 minutes, stirring to dissolve crumbs. Allow to cool, then spread on bread and serve.

*Makes about 1½ quarts cheese*

# Cottage Cheese

1½ gallons milk
1 tsp. salt
½ cup fresh cream

Let milk sour until it is very thick. Heat to 115° – 120°, then put into coarse cloth bag and allow to drain overnight.

When curds are dry, crumble until fine and mix in the salt thoroughly.

When ready to serve, stir in the fresh cream and combine well.

*Makes about 3½ cups cheese*

# Egg Cheese

2 quarts fresh milk
5 eggs
2 cups buttermilk or sour milk
1 tsp. salt
1 tsp. sugar

Heat fresh milk to the boiling point.

Beat eggs until lemon-colored. Add buttermilk or sour milk, salt and sugar. Beat just until mixed, then pour slowly into the hot fresh milk. Cover and let set for 5 minutes.

Stir mixture until curds and whey separate. With a slotted spoon lift the curds into a mold with drainage holes on the bottom. Layer the curds into the mold lightly to prevent the cheese from packing heavily together.

When thoroughly cooled the cheese can be sliced out of the container or unmolded onto a dish and served as a spread for bread.

# Cup Cheese

2½ gallons milk
1½ tsp. baking soda
1½ tsp. salt
½ cup water

Let milk sour until it is very thick. Heat to 120°, pour into a coarse cloth bag and let drain overnight.

Crumble curds until they are fine, then mix soda with cheese thoroughly. Place in bowl, cover with a cloth and let set at room temperature for 3 days. Stir every morning and evening.

At the end of the third day, place the bowl of cheese in the upper part of a double boiler. Over heat, stir in salt and water until smooth. Cheese should be thick and yellow, and have a sharp smell.

Pour into cup-size containers. Cool, then spread on bread to serve. (Some folks like to drizzle molasses or honey over the cheese before eating.)

# Beverages

Steamy hot days in the hay fields are brightened by a delegation from the kitchen bringing icy lemonade and peppermint water.

Long afternoons in the garden are rewarded with fresh meadow tea.

Summer evenings stretch into darkness with pretzels and homemade root beer.

Cooler days bring apple cider.

Resourceful cooks, most Amish women still depend upon their gardens and orchards when making drinks for their families. Root beer mix and lemons come from the grocery store, but apart from those purchased products, the preparation is traditionally from scratch.

# Fresh Meadow Tea

Multiple varieties of tea grow in meadows, gardens and flower beds in eastern Pennsylvania. The leaves can be used fresh, dried or frozen.

Many cooks keep a gallon jar of fresh tea in the refrigerator from May through September. They also see to it that tea leaves and stems are laid out on paper to dry in a little used corner of the house. (It's a way to insure a supply of meadow tea for hot drinks in the wintertime.) Those with access to a freezer have discovered the convenience of mixing up a tea concentrate and freezing it for some future occasion when time or the season does not allow making it with fresh leaves.

1 cup sugar
1 pint water
1 cup fresh tea leaves, either peppermint or spearmint
juice of 1 lemon
water

Stir sugar and pint of water together in a saucepan and bring to a boil.

Pour boiling syrup over tea leaves and let steep for 20 minutes. Remove the leaves and let tea cool.

Add the lemon juice and enough water to make ½ gallon of tea. Serve either hot or cold.

*Makes ½ gallon*

# Frozen Meadow Tea Concentrate

2 cups sugar (or less)
5 cups water
1 large handful garden tea
1 cup lemon juice
1 cup orange juice
water

Boil sugar in 5 cups water. Pour over garden tea. Cover and steep for 1 hour.

Remove tea. Add juices. Freeze.

*Note:* This makes a concentrate which must be diluted with 2 parts water to 1 part concentrate.

*Makes about 6 quarts*

# Root Beer

1 tsp. dry yeast
½ cup warm water
2 cups granulated sugar
1 quart hot water
4 tsp. root beer extract

Dissolve yeast in ½ cup warm water.

Dissolve sugar in 1 quart hot water.

Mix together dissolved yeast, sugar and root beer extract in gallon jar. Fill jar with warm water and stir until all ingredients are well combined.

Cover jar. Set in warm sun for four hours. The root beer will be ready to drink the next day. Chill before serving.

*Makes 1 gallon root beer*

# Lemonade

Never mind that lemons didn't grow in Pennsylvania's orchards. "We got lemons at the store when I was a girl," states a woman in her 50s. "We always had lemons in the summer for lemonade." Relatively accessible and economical, the fruit brought variety to the hot-weather drink repertoire.

> 4 lemons
> 3 cups sugar
> 1 quart hot water
> 3 quarts cold water

Wash and slice lemons. Remove seeds. Stomp lemon slices and sugar together with a potato masher until well mixed.

Add hot water to lemon and sugar mixture and stir to dissolve sugar and extract the lemon pulp and juice.

Squeeze lemon slices by hand to get balance of juice before disposing of slices. Add cold water to mixture and stir until well blended. Chill and serve.

*Makes 1 gallon*

# Grape Juice Concentrate

Grapes, especially the Concord variety, grow bountifully on arbors and fences on many Amish farms.

Grape juice is served fresh in season; it is canned, often in concentrate form, for sharing with visitors and at special times throughout the year.

> 10 lbs. grapes
> 2 cups water
> 1½ lbs. sugar

Wash grapes, add water and cook until soft. Put through fruit press until juice stops flowing.

Add sugar and stir until dissolved.

Bring juice to a boil, then pour into jars and bottles and seal.

To serve, mix grape juice concentrate with an equal amount of water.

# Eggnog

When eggs, milk and cream are plentiful, eggnog does not need to be restricted to Christmastime. One respected cook explained, "We made eggnog fairly often. In fact, we had it more throughout the year than at holiday time when there were other goodies around. Of course we had the milk and eggs—and my dad had ulcers, so he drank eggnog for his stomach."

**4 eggs**
**⅓ cup granulated sugar**
**⅛ tsp. nutmeg**
**dash of salt**
**4 Tbsp. lemon juice or 2 Tbsp. apple cider vinegar mixed**
    **with 2 Tbsp. water**
**4 cups cold milk**
**½ cup cold cream**

Beat eggs until thick. Mix in sugar, seasonings and lemon juice or vinegar.

Add cold milk and cream, then beat until frothy. Serve immediately.

*Makes 6 large cups*

# Peppermint Drink

To avoid dehydration for the farmhands during hot summer days in the fields, cooks derived vinegar punch, soda water and peppermint drink. The chemical combinations quenched thirsts more effectively than fruit drinks and eased stomachs threatened by the heat.

**2 quarts ice water**
**½ cup sugar**
**a few drops essence of peppermint or peppermint spirits**

Combine all ingredients and mix well. Serve ice cold.

*Makes 8 servings*

# Tomato Juice Cocktail

This thick, flavorful drink has become an additional reason for raising tomatoes. The fruit is a staple in the Amish diet, in many forms—sliced fresh, stewed, made into multiple baked dishes, and cooked into soup.

This basic recipe is itself healthily versatile. It can be drunk as an appetizer or snack; it can form the basis of a well spiced soup.

½ bushel tomatoes
3 stalks celery (leaves and all)
3 large onions
6 medium carrots
3 green peppers
a little water
1 cup sugar
2 Tbsp. salt

Cut raw vegetables into 1″ pieces. Put all together into large stockpot. Add water to a depth of 1 inch. Cook slowly until soft, then put through food press.

To pureed mixture add sugar and salt. Bring to a boil. Pour into jars and seal.

# Spiced Cider

Commercial cider presses were begun to meet the local demand for cider-making. Family orchards and local fruit farms cover the land from the central counties of Pennsylvania on eastward.

The apple drink is most often served cold, but in recent years it has become a well liked hot drink, especially as winter comes and the cider season ends.

  1 gallon apple cider
  1 cup orange juice
  1 Tbsp. lemon juice
  3 cinnamon sticks
  1 tsp. allspice
  1 tsp. ground cloves
  sugar to taste

Mix all ingredients except sugar together. Taste and add sugar if needed.

Bring to a boil and simmer gently for 6–8 minutes. Strain and serve hot.

*Makes 16–17 cups of cider*

# Candies

The Amish, in general, like sweets. Fancy confections are not a part of their cooking tradition, however. There has never been time for such fuss on Amish farms. Furthermore, in the early years of the Pennsylvania settlement, sugar was a precious commodity. It tended to be used first for canning fruits, pickled relishes and jams and jellies. Pies and cakes were the next priority. If sugar could be spared, candy was made now and then.

Candy production seldom happened except at Christmastime or in the late fall for special young people's gatherings. Taffy pulls were social occasions for Amish teenagers growing up at the beginning of this century. It's a tradition that still lives, although the candy ingredients may vary from those used eighty years ago.

With candy so easily and economically available now, few cooks invest time and energy in making their own. Several women in their middle 30s and 40s remember little candymaking during their childhoods. "At Christmastime we'd spread peanut butter and marshmallow on saltines or graham crackers, then dip them in melted chocolate," explained one. Another said that occasionally she spreads store-bought snack crackers with peanut butter and coats them with chocolate.

Two grandmothers in their late 50s reflected another era. "I remember we made fudge, but mostly at Christmas. When I was real young, chocolate wasn't that available so we didn't melt it and use it for coating."

The other grandmother recalled making candy only at

Christmas. Although they made fudge, "Melinda candy" is what she remembers most vividly. "It was a sugar, corn syrup and water mixture, probably given that name because the recipe came from a woman named Melinda!"

Candymaking is still a rare activity, done most often, it seems, as a kind of celebration or way to have fun. Here are some of the traditional recipes from the generations of Amish families who have made their homes in eastern Pennsylvania.

# Taffy

1 cup sugar
¾ cup light corn syrup
⅔ cup water
1 Tbsp. cornstarch
2 Tbsp. butter
1 tsp. salt
2 tsp. vanilla

Mix together all ingredients except vanilla. Stir over low heat until sugar is dissolved. Bring to boil, without stirring further, until mixture reaches the hard ball stage (265° — when a small piece dropped into cold water forms a hard ball).

Remove from heat, stir in vanilla and pour into buttered pan.

Butter hands. When taffy is cool enough to handle (but not too cool!), cut in long pieces and pull with a partner until candy becomes satiny, stiff and light in color. Finished strips should be about ½″ wide. Cut in 1½″ lengths and wrap individual pieces in waxed paper.

# Old-Fashioned Molasses Taffy

2 cups molasses
1 cup sugar
1 cup milk
1 Tbsp. vinegar
2 Tbsp. butter
1 tsp. baking soda

Mix together all ingredients except baking soda. Stir over low heat until sugar is dissolved. Bring to boil, without stirring further, until it reaches hard ball stage (265° — when a small piece dropped into cold water forms a hard ball).

Remove from heat and stir in soda. Pour into long buttered baking pan.

Butter hands. When taffy is cool enough to handle (it may still cause blisters!), cut off long pieces and pull with partner until it becomes satiny, stiff and light in color. Finished strips should be about ½″ wide. Cut in 1½″ lengths and wrap individual pieces in waxed paper.

# Fudge

4 Tbsp. cocoa (or 3 squares unsweetened baker's chocolate)
3 cups sugar
1 cup milk or cream
3 Tbsp. corn syrup
pinch of salt
2 Tbsp. butter
2 tsp. vanilla

Combine cocoa, sugar, milk, syrup and salt in heavy saucepan. Cook to soft ball stage (236° — when small amount of mixture dropped in cold water forms a soft ball).

Cool slightly and add butter and vanilla. Immediately pour into buttered pan. Allow to harden. Cut into squares.

*Makes about 2 lbs.*

# Chocolate Fudge with Nuts

⅓ cup butter
3 squares unsweetened chocolate
¼ cup milk
3 cups confectioner's sugar, sifted
pinch of salt
1 tsp. vanilla
¼ cup nuts, chopped

Melt butter and chocolate in saucepan. Add milk slowly, stirring continuously until well blended. Remove from heat.

Gradually beat in sugar. Stir in salt, vanilla and nuts until thoroughly mixed.

Spread in greased 8″ square pan. Chill. When firm, cut in 1″ pieces.

*Makes 64 1″ pieces*

# Peanut Brittle

2 cups granulated sugar
1 cup white corn syrup
½ cup boiling water
3 cups salted peanuts
2 tsp. baking soda

Combine sugar, corn syrup and water in a heavy 4-quart pan. Stir over heat only until the sugar is dissolved. Cook until mixture reaches the soft-ball stage (236°).

Add the peanuts. Cook until mixture becomes golden brown and reaches the hardcrack stage (290°), stirring occasionally. Remove from heat and stir in soda thoroughly.

Pour at once onto buttered cookie sheet. Spread to a thin layer. Cool, then break into pieces.

# Caramel Corn

5 quarts popped corn
2 cups granulated sugar
¾ cup white corn syrup
2 Tbsp. vinegar
2 Tbsp. water
1 tsp. baking soda
1 cup peanuts, whole or chopped

Warm popped corn in slow oven. Meanwhile, heat the sugar over low heat, allowing it to brown but not scorch. Add syrup, vinegar, water and salt to it. Stir only until sugar is dissolved. Boil mixture until it forms a hard ball when it is dropped in cold water (270°).

Remove from heat and add soda and peanuts, stirring well. Pour immediately over warm popped corn.

Stir well until all kernels are coated. Allow to cool, stirring occasionally to break up large chunks.

# Popcorn Balls

3 quarts popped corn
1 cup sugar
½ cup corn syrup, white or dark
⅓ cup water
¼ cup butter
¾ tsp. salt
¾ tsp. vanilla

Warm popped corn in slow oven. Meanwhile, combine over heat in saucepan the sugar, corn syrup, water, butter and salt. Stir until the sugar is dissolved.

Cook without stirring until the syrup forms a soft ball (236°). Then add the vanilla and pour the syrup slowly over the popped corn. Mix well so that every kernel is coated.

Grease hands well with butter before shaping sticky popcorn into balls.

*Makes 12 medium-sized balls*

# Caramels

1 cup granulated sugar
½ cup brown sugar
½ cup light corn syrup
½ cup cream
¾ cup milk
¼ cup butter
½ cup nuts, chopped (optional)
1 tsp. vanilla

Combine all ingredients except vanilla and cook over low heat, stirring constantly, until candy forms a firm ball when dropped into cold water (246°).

Stir in vanilla, then pour into a greased, 8″ square baking pan.

Cool, then turn out of pan and cut candy into 1″ pieces. Wrap each square in waxed paper.

*Makes 64 1″ pieces*

# Hickory Nut Candy

Hickory nut trees once populated the fencerows and roadsides of rural eastern Pennsylvania. Their nuts were special treats to flavor cakes and candy.

1½ cups sugar
1 cup sweet milk
⅓ cup hickory nuts, chopped
1 tsp. vanilla
1 Tbsp. butter, softened

Mix together sugar, milk and nuts over medium heat, stirring only until sugar is dissolved. Bring to boil, without stirring further, until a soft ball is formed when small amount of mixture is dropped into cold water (236°).

Remove from heat and add vanilla and butter. Beat together until fluffy. Spoon into 8″ square baking pan. Chill. When firm, cut into 1″ squares.

*Makes 64 1″ squares*

# Hard Tack Candy

An old recipe, reminiscent of Melinda Candy (see page 204)!

3½ cups granulated sugar
1 cup water
1 cup light corn syrup
food coloring
flavoring

Combine sugar, water and syrup and cook until candy is
brittle when dropped in cold water (280°). Stir in food coloring,
leaving mixture on heat until it reaches 290°.

Remove from heat and add ⅛ ounce of desired flavoring
(peppermint, spearmint, cinnamon, wintergreen, anise, etc.).

Pour immediately onto greased cookie sheet. When cooled,
cut into bite-sized pieces with scissors.

# Kisses

Coconuts could be bought at the turn of the century in eastern
Pennsylvania. They were, of course, in their hard shells, leaving it
up to the enterprising cook (or her helpers) to ferret out their meat
and grate it. Coconut was a delicacy in cakes, cracker puddings
and, on occasion, candy.

3 egg whites
2 cups plus 1 Tbsp. sugar
2 tsp. vinegar
1 tsp. vanilla
2 cups flaked coconut

Beat egg whites till frothy. Gradually add sugar and vinegar.
Beat until fluffy (about 10 minutes). Stir in vanilla and coconut.

Drop by teaspoons onto cookie sheets. Bake at 250° for
30–45 minutes.

*Variation:*
Crushed nuts may be substituted for coconut.

*Makes about 2 lbs.*

# O. Henry Candy

*Part 1*

>   2 cups granulated sugar
>   1 cup light corn syrup
>   1 cup water
>   ¾ cup peanut butter

Combine over heat, stirring only until sugar is dissolved. Cook until hard ball stage (265°). Let cool, then add peanut butter. Stir thoroughly. Shape into rolls ¾″ thick and 1″ long. Set aside.

*Part 2*

>   1 cup light corn syrup
>   ½ cup brown sugar
>   2 lbs. of peanuts, chopped fine
>   8 oz. dipping chocolate

Cook corn syrup and sugar together until hard ball stage (265°). Then dip candy from Part 1 into this and roll in peanuts while still hot.

Melt dipping chocolate in top of double boiler. Dip rolls into melted chocolate and drop on waxed paper.

# Menus for Special Occasions

Major community events have been critical in the maintenance of the Amish food tradition. All of these occasions are held in homes.

A family planning a wedding or suddenly facing a funeral knows what guests expect and takes comfort in that. A standard meal for Sunday lunch simplifies that aspect of the hosts' preparation and reduces possible temptations to be competitive.

For a people reluctant to express their feelings verbally, food becomes a way to show affection, sympathy, gratitude. Food supports these gathered occasions.

The menus which follow are typical, contemporary ones served in Lancaster County, Pennsylvania. Elements may vary from family to family and according to the seasons.

# A Wedding Dinner
# for 300 people

32 chickens for the Roast
38 loaves of bread for the Roast filling
4 buckets of potatoes for Mashed Potatoes
10 quarts of Gravy
¾ bushel of cabbage for Cole Slaw
Creamed Celery
25 quarts of Applesauce
30 loaves of Bread
12 pounds of Butter
20 quarts of Canned Peaches
20 quarts of Canned Pears
15 quarts of Spiced Cantaloupe
22 dozen Doughnuts
10 pounds of confectioner's sugar (in which doughnuts
   are dipped)
30 Custard pies
30 Fruit Pies with lattice tops
5 Layer Cakes
2 lard cans of Sugar Cookies and others
5 or 6 lard cans of Potato Chips
4 pounds of regular coffee or 2 large jars of instant coffee

# A Wedding Supper

20 Chickens to stew, or an equivalent amount of legs and
   thighs to bake
½ lard can of Wafers (over which the chicken is ladled)
1½ bushels of Sweet Potatoes for frying
14 quarts of milk for Cornstarch
Pies
Cakes
Cookies

# Sunday Lunch
# following Church, served by the host family
# to about 200 people (70 – 100 of
# whom are adults)

25 loaves of homemade Bread

3 pounds of Butter for the bread

3 pints of Jelly

1¼ gallons of Church Spread (1 gallon of molasses, 1 pint of smooth peanut butter, 1 pint of marshmallow cream)

¾ bucket of Schmierkase *or* cubes of cheese cut from 2 large rolls of either longhorn or muenster cheese

5 quarts of Pickles (may be 2 different kinds)

5 quarts of Pickled Red Beets

40 Schnitz Pies

Coffee and Tea

Chocolate Milk (Served only if the family chooses, if they live on a farm and the weather is hot.)

The above amounts may vary depending upon the weather and its effect on appetites. Furthermore, if the members of a church district are quite scattered and have long distances to travel to church, they may eat more at lunch than those who live comparatively close to each other. In some cases families may rise as early as 3:00 a.m. to do their milking and barn chores and be at church by 8:30 a.m. Frequently they do not have time for a full breakfast.

# A Funeral Dinner
# for 75 people

30 pounds of rolled Roast Beef (to be baked, then sliced
and served cold)

2 buckets of potatoes for Mashed Potatoes

Gravy

10 loaves of Bread

10 dozen Rolls

5 pounds of Butter and Jelly

Cole Slaw

Cheese Cubes (from 1 large roll of longhorn cheese and 2
large rolls of muenster cheese)

8 pounds of Prunes (to be stewed, then served cold.
Depending upon the season and situation, fresh or
canned fruit may be served instead.)

1 large jar of Coffee

Pies and Cakes (these are brought by the guests, rather
than being supplied by the family.)

# Endnotes

[1] Don Yoder, "Historical Sources for American Traditional Cookery: Examples from the Pennsylvania German Culture," *Pennsylvania Folklife* 20 (Fall, 1969), p. 25.

[2] William Woys Weaver, *Sauerkraut Yankees* (Philadelphia: University of Pennsylvania Press, 1983), pp. 19, 20.

[3] Ibid., pp. 21, 22.

[4] Ibid., pp. 151, 152.

[5] Ibid.

[6] Ibid., p. 116.

[7] Ibid., p. 103.

[8] Ibid., pp. 151, 152.

# Readings and Sources

## Cooking

*Favorite Amish Family Recipes.* Aylmer, Ontario: Pathway Publishing House, 1965.

Gehris, Elda F. "Pennsylvania German Cookery," *Pennsylvania Folklife* 35 (Fall, 1985) 1, 35–48.

Good, Phyllis Pellman. *Cooking and Memories.* Intercourse, Pennsylvania: Good Books, 1983.

Good, Phyllis Pellman and Rachel Thomas Pellman. *From Amish and Mennonite Kitchens.* Intercourse, Pennsylvania: Good Books, 1984.

Groff, Betty and José Wilson. *Good Earth and Country Cooking.* Harrisburg: Stackpole Books, 1974.

Hark, Ann and Preston Barba. *Pennsylvania Dutch Cookery: A Regional Cookbook.* Allentown, Pennsylvania, 1950.

Lapp, Sallie Y. and Sylvia Y. Miller. *Lancaster County Amish Cookbook.* Bird-in-Hand and New Holland, Pennsylvania: Miller and Lapp, 1982.

Lehman, David J., editor. *Der Dutchman Amish Kitchen Cooking Cookbook.* Berlin, Ohio: The Gospel Book Store, 1972.

Lemon, James T. "Household Consumption in 18th Century America and Its Relationship to Production and Trade: The Situation Among Farmers in Southeastern Pennsylvania," *Agricultural History* 41 (January, 1967), 59–70.

Long, Amos, Jr. "Bakeovens in the Pennsylvania Folk Culture," *Pennsylvania Folklife* 14 (December 1964), 16–29.

Lund, Adrienne F. *The Amish Way Cookbook.* Louisville, Kentucky: Edward D. Donahoe, 1981.

Miller, Bob and Sue, editors. *Amish-Country Cookbook, Volume*

*I.* Elkhart, Indiana: Bethel Publishing, 1979.

——— *Amish-Country Cookbook, Volume II.* Elkhart, Indiana: Bethel Publishing, 1986.

Miller, Mark Eric, editor. *Amish Cooking.* Scottdale, Pennsylvania: Herald Press, 1980.

Schrock, Johnny, editor. *Wonderful Good Cooking from Amish Country Kitchens.* Scottdale, Pennsylvania: Herald Press, 1974.

Showalter, Mary Emma. *Mennonite Community Cookbook.* Scottdale, Pennsylvania: Herald Press, 1950.

Weaver, William Woys. *Sauerkraut Yankees, Pennsylvania German Foods and Foodways.* Philadelphia: University of Pennsylvania Press, 1983.

Yoder, Don. "Historical Sources for American Traditional Cookery: Examples from the Pennsylvania German Culture," *Pennsylvania Folklife* 20 (Spring, 1971), 16–29.

——— "Pennsylvanians Call It Mush," *Pennsylvania Folklife* 13 (Winter, 1962–1963), 27–49.

——— "Sauerkraut in the Pennsylvania Folk Culture," *Pennsylvania Folklife* 12 (Summer, 1961), 56–69.

——— "Schnitz in the Pennsylvania Folk Culture," *Pennsylvania Folklife* 12 (Fall, 1961), 44–53.

## About the People

Bender, H. S. *The Anabaptist Vision.* Scottdale, Pennsylvania: Herald Press, 1944.

Dyck, Cornelius J. *An Introduction to Mennonite History.* Scottdale, Pennsylvania: Herald Press, 1967.

Good, Merle. *Who Are the Amish?* Intercourse, Pennsylvania: Good Books, 1985.

——— and Phyllis. *Twenty Most Asked Questions about the Amish and Mennonites.* Intercourse, Pennsylvania: Good Books, 1979.

Hostetler, John A. *Amish Society.* Baltimore: Johns Hopkins University Press, 1968.

Kaiser, Grace. *Dr. Frau: A Woman Doctor Among the Amish.* Intercourse, Pennsylvania: Good Books, 1986.

McCauley, Daniel and Kathryn. *Decorative Arts of the Amish of Lancaster County.* Intercourse, Pennsylvania: Good Books, 1988.

Pellman, Rachel and Kenneth. *The World of Amish Quilts.* Intercourse, Pennsylvania: Good Books, 1984.

# Index

Phyllis Pellman Good, a Lancaster County, Pennsylvania, native, first discovered that she was a Pennsylvania Dutch cook when she drew a curious audience in a dorm kitchen in New York City one evening while preparing Chicken Corn Soup. She has since authored *Cooking and Memories* and *The Festival Cookbook,* and co-authored *From Amish and Mennonite Kitchens.*

Today Phyllis spends much of her time as a book editor. She also edits *Festival Quarterly,* a magazine exploring the art, faith and culture of Mennonite peoples. She is co-editor of the book *Perils of Professionalism* and co-editor with her husband, Merle, of *20 Most Asked Questions about the Amish and Mennonites.*

Together she and Merle are executive directors of The People's Place, The Old Country Store and several associated shops in Intercourse, Pennsylvania.

Phyllis received her B.A. and M.A. in English from New York University.

The Goods are parents of two daughters and members of the Landisville Mennonite Church, Landisville, Pennsylvania.